JORDEN BEACON

Financial Outlook

A Beginner Guide to Economics Independence

Copyright © 2024 by Jorden Beacon

All rights reserved. No part of this publication may be reproduced, stored or transmitted in any form or by any means, electronic, mechanical, photocopying, recording, scanning, or otherwise without written permission from the publisher. It is illegal to copy this book, post it to a website, or distribute it by any other means without permission.

First edition

Contents

1 Introduction	1
2 Financial Thinking	3
Psychology of Money	3
Good Financial Habits	6
Six Kinds of Fear by Napoleon Hill	10
3 The Essence of Money	17
The Essence of goods and money	17
Basic Functions of Money	18
The History of Money	20
Time Value of Money	22
Inflation	24
Types of money	28
4 Financial Planning and Accounting	32
Financial planning of the organization	33
Personal financial planning	37
Five Steps to Financial Planning	40
Programs for planning a personal budget	44
5 Financial Analysis	47
Financial Analysis Tools	48
Financial stability analysis	50
Solvency and liquidity analysis	50
Investment Analysis	51
Bankruptcy probability analysis	52
Business market value analysis	53
Break Even	55

Stock Exchanges	55
Dow Jones Industrial Average	58
6 Investing and Saving	60
Cash Flow Quadrant	62
Credit as an ambiguous income generator	64
Assets and liabilities	66
Warren Buffett's investing rules	67
Sources of passive and conditionally passive income	72
7 The Power of Positive Thinking	80
Practice positive thinking	81
8 Mastering Money Habits	83
9 Fixed Mindset	89
A Step-by-Step Process for Changing a Fixed Mindset	90
10 Money Management	94
Excuses for Financial illiteracy	94
How to learn to manage money	96
Set financial goals	98
How to learn to save money	99
How to get rid of debts	102
11 Wealth-Building Strategies	105
Analyze the situation and surroundings	106
Identify Strategic Options	107
Evaluate and select the best strategic options	108
12 Bad Financial Habits	110
13 Financial Literacy	115
14 Personal Budget Management Tips	119
What is Budget?	120
Accounting for income and expenses	121
Cost optimization	122
15 Mutual Funds	124
Types of Mutual Funds	125

Investing in Mutual Funds	126
16 Convert your Abilities into Money	128
Summarize	129
Step Two: Pay Attention to Your Environment and Look for Opportunities	129
Step Three: Create a Plan to Address the Opportunity You've Identified	130
Step Four: Develop a Process to Put the Plan into Action	131
17 10 mistakes of a New Entrepreneur	133
18 Financial Problem and their Solution	139
Solution of Financial Problem	141
19 How to Overcome the Fear of Failure and Develop a Growth...	147
The Need for Failure	148
The Importance of Mentality	149
How to overcome the fear of failure and develop a growth mentality in your organization	150
Together we make mistakes and together we win	152
20 Review Request	154

1

Introduction

"**Financial Outlook**" isn't just about numbers and spreadsheets. It's about rewiring your thinking, befriending your finances, and finally feeling empowered, not overwhelmed, by money. We'll dive into the psychology of spending, expose spending traps, and equip you with tools to make smart choices, every time.

Everything comes from the head. You need to develop a financial mindset to get your feet on the ground financially and make intuitive entrepreneurial decisions. Of course, it is possible to invade the world of big money and business with the old psychology and even succeed in it, but let's do it wisely.

The thinking of a poor person is different from the thinking of a rich person. To quote writer Jerry Gullies:

> "**The more you focus on not having enough money, the less money you will have. Poverty comes to those who are emotionally and intellectually ready to accept it.**"

FINANCIAL OUTLOOK

Thoughts, emotions, fears, and rules shape human thinking, so we will focus on all of these elements.

To instill a financial mindset in yourself, you need to learn three important elements. And the first of these will be understanding the psychology of money. Financial thinking has a lot to do with how we think about money. And these feelings can have a big impact on our financial success.

Many people think that the psychology of money is a conventional term with nothing behind it. This is a new direction in psychology, which is being studied by scientists, financiers, and psychologists from all over the world.

Stop wishing for financial freedom and start building it! "Financial Mindset 101" is your road map to a richer, happier you. Grab your copy and get ready to say "hello" to financial harmony and "goodbye" to money meltdowns!

2

Financial Thinking

Financial thinking is a person's way of perceiving the world and himself in it in terms of income and expenses.

We know that money is pure energy that you need to be able to work with to succeed financially and transform reality. A person's thinking, including financial thinking, is the basis of his life, on which social connections, relationships with the outside world, the ability to present himself, material status, etc. are built.

Correct financial thinking will always lead a person to the right path, no matter how hard it may be for him at some point in life. It is always based on the desire to create, self-confidence, and the belief that the Universe provides a sea of opportunities that can be used.

Psychology of Money

The psychology of money is a branch of psychology that studies a person's attitude toward money and towards other people in connection with money relations, as well as the influence of monetary factors on human behavior, in particular on decision-making.

"The latest research shows that the biological mechanisms of the brain play an important role in the theme of "Man and Money." Human behavior in financial matters is quite predictable, although this may not correspond to the patterns of classical economic theories" (The Psychology Money, M. Argyle, A. Furnham).

Among the predictable psychological effects, the following were identified :

Money Illusion. This is a person's tendency to perceive a nominal rather than a real amount of money. Those. a person does not adjust for inflation, even if he knows about it.

Money Taboo. Some cultures prohibit the use of money in certain situations, even if it is economically desirable.

Monetary Conservatism. This is resistance to any monetary reforms.

Silencing Effect. In some families and cultures, it is not common to talk about money. This topic is considered indecent for discussion. When a person breaks out of such a society, he begins to raise the topic of money, protesting against his **Upbringing.** This leads to the fact that such behavior is condemned by the new society because it has developed a more correct discourse on the topic of money and does not tolerate the empty mention of it.

The effect of money tension. This is an emotional relationship between people about money. The topic of money provokes very strong, sometimes even affective, emotions: love and hatred, envy and sacrifice. Most people develop an ambiguous, contrasting attitude towards money.

The effect of the illusion of material money. Money is classified as material, although in essence, it has not been such for a long time - ever since it ceased to have independent value. The evolution from commodity to fiat money has meant that it continues to be considered something material, and this leads to many psychological problems and cognitive dissonance.

The effect of different money. People treat different types of money differently, and this is a very interesting paradox. Spending money with a bank card is considered more painless than in cash, although they are the same thing. Coins weigh more than banknotes and are even harder to part with. People consider some types of money to be dirty, immoral, and evil, while others are good, easy, and reliable.

The effect of monetary profanation. If a person gets money through hard and unpleasant work, it becomes something vulgar and negative for him. He looks at money and sees not opportunity, but suffering and hard work. While easy money is spent quickly, people part with it without regret.

The lending effect. Borrowing money is morally condemned and at the same time lending is approved. At different times, attitudes towards these processes have changed. Nowadays, debt is considered a source of stress and new forms of behavior.

Money size effect. They don't raise small change, but they try to hide large sums. For many people, there is a certain threshold amount after which their behavior changes significantly.

The effect of individual economic behavior. Individual economic behavior differs significantly from the behavior of groups and organizations.

The effect of the superior value of money. The transfer of money in exchange for goods is much simpler than the exchange of goods for money. We have already talked about the high liquidity of money - it can be exchanged for anything. Therefore, a sum of money is more valuable than a commodity of similar value.

The effect of monetary arithmetic. Logical-mathematical operations (addition, division, subtraction) with money and abstract numbers have their own distinct rules, norms, and psychological attitudes toward them.

These patterns are worth knowing for any person who wants to learn to think in financial terms. As you may have noticed, most of the above-presented misconceptions that are characteristic of poor people. A rich person does not have such thinking; he knows the true value of money and very rarely allows himself to be fooled. All other people are forced to endure all these monetary paradoxes until they are recognized and eradicated.

The development of financial thinking is influenced by financial habits, and this is the second element on the path to achieving it. They help you get rid of constant financial stress and begin to view money as a tool for achieving freedom, and not as an end in itself. To grow them and introduce them into your subconscious, a certain amount of time must pass. Therefore, we will consider each of them separately, find out why they work, and begin to cultivate them in our own country.

Good Financial Habits

Pay yourself first

This is a habit that was developed and voiced by Robert Kiyosaki and which is observed in the vast majority of millionaires around the world. Renowned financial writer Dave Ramsey notes: "Saving just $100 a month from age 25 to age 65 at 12% interest is $1,176,000. Anyone can retire a millionaire!

Some experts recommend the 50-30-20 rule: spend 50% of your income on necessities (food, rent, rent), 30% on everything you want, and 20% on saving and investing. Use this rule for all your income. Better yet, save 50% if you can.

Have a financial goal

We touched on this habit in the second lesson, when we talked about financial planning, but it wouldn't hurt to remind you. According to a study by Thomas Corley, 81% of millionaires have a clear financial plan and stick to it, while only 9% of middle-income people do the same.

Most successful people first set themselves a simple goal: "Make a million," and having achieved this, they began to set more ambitious goals - investing and diversifying income.

Find your goal and make a financial plan.

Be comfortable with uncertainty

This is another habit that financially illiterate people are least likely to adhere to. Millionaires know how to take risks and feel confident in any development of events. Tony Robbins, a famous motivational speaker, said: "Life is all about uncertainty. Quality of life is determined by the amount of uncertainty you can handle. Develop self-confidence, gain experience, and be more flexible. You will never know what will happen."

Psychologically, uncertainty can lead to fear, which, in turn, leads to acquired helplessness, and reluctance to take action even in favorable conditions. Therefore, the ability to be calm and self-confident in matters of a vague future is so important in financial matters.

Chat with millionaires

This may seem like mocking advice, but if you think about it a little, you will realize that there are professions that contribute to this. For example, journalists or writers can interview rich people and even make acquaintances with them.

Tony Robbins defends his point of view on this, saying that people of the same profession attract each other. The same is true for financially literate people. Now this is called networking and enough books have been written on this topic so that everyone can express themselves in this type of activity.

The author of five books on financial independence, Grant Cardon, writes: "People who don't have their own money are unable to teach you how to earn it. You should know what millionaires do to create their wealth. What are their habits? What are they reading? How do they invest? What controls them? How do they motivate themselves?

Don't waste time on the Internet and TV

According to the same study by Thomas Corley, 76% of poor people spend more than five hours a day watching TV or using the Internet without any benefit, while 60% of millionaires spend less than an hour on this. Rich people are always busy doing useful things, while poor people are simply always busy doing something. And this significant difference costs the other millions of dollars.

You may debate whether this is a financial habit, but any successful person will tell you that time is money. Don't waste it.

Create several sources of income

We touched on this topic in the fourth lesson. Rich people rarely get their money from just one source. They accumulate and invest, and so on in a circle.

Rich people know firsthand about financial risks, so they insure themselves by creating multiple sources of income for themselves. This rule may have no place in love relationships, but in financial relationships it is golden.

Buy wisely

Rich people very rarely make rash purchases because they know how business and advertising work. Of course, we are talking about those people who earned their fortune themselves. They buy exactly as much as they need - for their needs and their business. These are the people who distinguish price from value. They can afford a lot of unnecessary purchases, but they know what this can lead to, because they are poor and remember that that habit kept them in this state for a long time.

Emotional spending can keep you at the bottom of a financial hole for a long time until you understand what it means to buy wisely. Instant satisfaction of needs is detrimental for any person in any area of life, but in the sphere of finance, it is doubly detrimental.

Get rid of the poor man's mentality

We are again touching on the psychological aspect of money matters. There is no shortage of money in the world, there is only a shortage of people who think about it correctly. To become a millionaire from scratch, you must get rid of the poor person's mindset. Such careful work on yourself will lead you to success in the foreseeable future.

Read as many books on finance as you can

Not all successful millionaires read a lot, that's true. This type of millionaire relies more on intuition than knowledge, but even they communicate with and listen to people who read a lot of books on finance.

If you can read seven books a month and pick up an idea from each one, imagine how many ideas you will have a few years later! The world is constantly changing and you need to feed yourself with important information every day. Read the books we recommend, then look for others. Just make it a habit to apply the tips and ideas from every book you read.

Napoleon Hill, in his best-selling book, **Think and Grow Rich**, lists six signs of fear. Knowing these signs will help not only in gaining financial independence but also in other aspects of life.

Six Kinds of Fear by Napoleon Hill

There are three enemies that every person should get rid of: fear, indecision, and doubt. Indecisiveness leads to doubt, which creates fear. And that, in turn, paralyzes a person's ability to act. Therefore, Napoleon Hill advises self-analysis to identify six signs of fear. To defeat an enemy, you need to know his name, habits, and habitat. Fear may be in your subconscious.

We have all been convinced more than once that thoughts tend to come true, so getting rid of fears will allow a person to gain financial success and thinking.

1). Fear of poverty

Many people are afraid of poverty and thereby bring it upon themselves. Here are six symptoms that will help you recognize this type of fear:

- **Indecisiveness** This is the habit of allowing others to think for themselves while remaining inactive.

- **Indifference** This is an unwillingness to fight poverty, an attitude toward a bad event as if it were fate, a lack of initiative, as well as intellectual and physical laziness.
- **Anxiety** A frowning, gloomy appearance, which leads to excessive alcohol consumption and addiction to drugs and smoking. Also, such people are characterized by self-doubt.
- **Doubt** manifests itself in the form of apologies and explanations.
- **Overcaution** Such people talk only about possible failures instead of focusing their minds on the means to achieve success. Pessimism leads to somatic diseases.
- **Procrastination** In our century this is called procrastination. Avoidance of responsibility and complete lack of initiative.

A person left without a job is ready to accept the first offer, which leads to a deterioration in his already terrible financial condition. He looks at the shop windows and feels like a second-class citizen. Envy exacerbates fear and helplessness. Fear of poverty breeds more poverty.

2). Fear of criticism

There is always enough criticism in our lives. It can cause an inferiority complex in a person and lead to a complete inability to build constructive relationships. It kills creative thinking and forces you to take several steps back.

Seven symptoms of fear of criticism:

Shyness Expressed in timidity and nervousness. It may seem like a pleasant character trait, but such a person is not capable of achieving success.

Weakness of character This is the thoughtless agreement with someone else's opinion and lack of ability to clearly express one's thoughts.

Imbalance Poor posture and memory, inability to control your voice and behavior. An extremely unpleasant character trait of a person who wants to devote his life to business.

Inferiority complex The habit of saying big words to impress. Such people seem self-confident, but in reality, they are not. They imitate others in the way they dress and speak, and are accustomed to inventing stories of their achievements.

Extravagance The desire to spend more than you have to appear richer, the habit of living beyond your means, and taking on debt.

Lack of self-esteem This is a habit of giving up any of your undertakings with a light heart, and laziness of soul and body.

Lack of initiative This is uncertainty in your ideas and fear of expressing your point of view.

Be careful when criticizing your child - this can lead to the problems described above. Learn to accept constructive criticism and be immune to unfounded criticism.

3). Fear of diseases

Fear of getting sick leads to somatic illnesses and makes a person weak in spirit. If you have this fear, you are unlikely to think about your financial success. Your head will be occupied with only one thing.

Fear of disease has seven symptoms :

Self-hypnosis. A person searches himself for symptoms of all possible diseases and, of course, finds them.

Hypochondria. Comes with bad thoughts. A person starts to get sick and sometimes even medications don't help.

Impressionability. It undermines the body's vital forces to resist.

Lethargy. This leads to excess weight and reluctance to do anything. In such a situation, a person is unable to motivate himself, much less think financially and look for sources of income.

Anxiety. A person reads medical literature, even if he is not sick, and constantly worries about himself.

Intemperance. This is the habit of drinking alcohol and nicotine instead of taking medications.
   Self-indulgence. The habit of arousing pity from others.

It may seem that the fear of illness and its manifestations are not directly related to financial independence. However, look at any millionaire - do you see at least one of these signs in him?

4). Fear of failure in love
This is perhaps a good fear when it comes to a poet and a creative person in general. But in financial matters, this is a destructive fear.

Three symptoms :

Jealousy. This is the habit of suspecting loved ones without any reason, complete disbelief, and suspicion.

Adventurism. Tendency to steal, cheat, and take risks. It's going into debt to buy gifts to show off your best side.

Finding mistakes in others. For the slightest reason.

5). Fear of old age

This fear comes from two sources. Firstly, from the idea that old age brings poverty. Secondly, from false beliefs that such a state is helpless and there is no joy in it.

Four symptoms:

"Forgive me, old man..." This is what some people say apologetically when they reach forty or fifty years of age.

Premature decline. By the age of forty, many people are finally overcome by an inferiority complex, which leads to the degradation of the human personality.

The desire to look younger. Imitating the clothes and behavior of young people, which looks ridiculous in the eyes of others.

Lack of initiative. If a person decides that he is old, it means that this quality is developing in him. He doesn't want to make any more serious decisions.

Only people who are unsure of their financial future, poor people are afraid of old age. The rich look at passing time differently, philosophically. They are not afraid of old age, they enjoy it. Some billionaires, even at 80 years old, work hard and find no reason for inaction and worry.

Fear of death

People fear death itself or for religious reasons. This often numbs such people so much that they are unable to think about anything else.

Three symptoms :

Thoughts about death These thoughts come to the minds of not only old people, but also young people, which prevents them from enjoying life. Often such thoughts come when a person has no meaning in life. Serving other people will help here - a person busy with other things will not think about death.

Connection with fear of poverty The death of a loved one is associated with the approach of one's poverty.

Connection with disease May lead to depression.

Napoleon Hill links all six types of fear to anxiety and asks how we can get rid of it. And Dale Carnegie, in his book " How to Stop Worrying, " answers this request.

We recommend that you read these two books from cover to cover because they contain a lot of important information. "Think and Grow Rich" will help you develop a financial mindset, and "How to Stop Worrying" will help you get rid of this unpleasant habit and eradicate fear.

And finally, I would like to warn you:

Humanity, represented by a huge number of people, commits a lot of stupid things. And if a crisis or something completely unexpected occurred in the world economy, this does not mean that it was deliberately provoked by someone. On the other hand, this also does not mean that someone did not make a big profit as a result of this

FINANCIAL OUTLOOK

event.

3

The Essence of Money

Financial literacy is impossible without understanding the essence of money and its properties. This topic is interesting and at the same time mandatory for every person who wants to learn how to handle them and understand by what laws they live. We encounter them every day and yet know absolutely nothing about them.

Money can be called the international language of the world market, in which people from all over the planet communicate. Understanding the functions of money is the first step to financial literacy. If you know the theory and understand the basics, you are armed with a tool that will help you learn how to manage them competently. Let's look at the history of the appearance of money, its functions, and its essence.

The Essence of goods and money

Money is impossible without goods. Therefore, first of all, you need to get a simple answer to the question: what is a product? A product is any product that meets three basic requirements:

1. Produced for sale
2. Satisfies specific needs
3. Has value

In this regard, the essence of money lies in the fact that it serves as an element and component of the economic activity of society, the relations between participants in the production process. Money is also a commodity (only universal) and therefore has the same properties as indicated above. But at the same time, they also have some unique properties. So what is money?

Maximum liquidity is characterized by the fact that you can easily exchange your money for goods, while the opposite is a rather problematic process for you. The closest synonyms for the term liquidity are marketability and ease of sale. In addition, money is:

- A tool for exchanging goods and services.
- A universal equivalent to the value of other goods and services.
- A kind of certification of the social nature of the private labor of the commodity producer.

Basic Functions of Money

With each new century, money acquires new specific functions, but some of them are universal. We will look at the:

The measure of value Money is capable of changing and measuring the value of a product, therefore it is a standard for it. The form of manifestation of the value of a product is price. Price is the cost of a product expressed in money. Because at the very beginning of its existence, money had an independent value (the silver and gold it contained), then initially the value of goods was correlated with the value of money through the ratio of social labor spent on their production. Nowadays, with the availability of loans, electronic money, and advertising funds, a lot has changed.

Sharing tool This is the original function of money, and it means that you can exchange your goods for money and then use it to purchase the goods you need. Over the millennia, dozens of others were added to this main function, completely changing the economic picture of the world.

Instrument of payment This function arose in connection with the development of credit relations. In this case, there is no reciprocal movement of money and goods. If you took out goods on credit, you will need to repay the amount of debt expressed in money, and not in goods. This function is also embodied in wages or making payments to the budget.

Means of circulation In this case, money acts as an intermediary in the circulation of goods. And this is where the liquidity indicator plays a key role. You can sell your goods today and buy raw materials whenever you want. A person can buy the goods he needs in one place and sell them in a completely different place, i.e. money overcomes spatial and temporal limitations.

Storage medium Not all money can and should be put into circulation immediately. A person can accumulate for a fairly long period, and then make some expensive purchase or order a service. The downside is that inflation is possible, which means the value of money will decrease.

World money Trade and loan relations were established between the countries of the world, which led to the emergence of the so-called world money. They function as a universal means of payment. Currently, five currencies are considered such: the US dollar, the euro, the Japanese yen, the British pound, and the Swiss franc. On October 1, 2016, the Chinese yuan became such a currency. However, people have learned to convert electronic money into 17 currencies, which significantly simplifies the process of commodity-market relations between countries.

As was said, the functions of money are constantly changing and supplemented, but the above ones have been universal for a long time. In connection with the emergence of new electronic money, as well as cryptocurrency, new functions may soon be invented, and along with them the essence of money itself will change.

The History of Money

Before the advent of money, the economy was significantly different from the modern one and functioned based on debt and gifts.

Some principles and elements of gifting still exist today, for example in the form of information. According to these principles, there is Wikipedia, torrent trackers, and with some exceptions, science. In this case, reputation and social position are acquired, which in the information world sometimes mean even more than the amount of money that can be earned by selling information. The desire to accumulate resources and information in the modern world is considered a sign of weakness and greed.

Then, in different regions of the world, people began to use various things as money:

✔ In many countries these were animal furs and skins, livestock.
  ✔ On the islands of Oceania, shells and pearls served as money.
  ✔ In New Zealand, stones with holes in the middle were used as money. The cost of such a stone was determined based on size, material, as well as its history. Some stones reached 3.6 meters in diameter.

✔In Kievan Rus, despite the monetary unit of the hryvnia, honey, salt, livestock, and animal furs were used.

✔Later, people began to use ingots, bars, and scraps of metal as money

As a result, the role of money shifted to metals. The function of money was performed by bronze, copper, iron, and silver. Over time, whole ingots of metal began to be used, which caused significant inconvenience because they had to be constantly weighed and the sample determined. Therefore, to avoid counterfeiting and overdressing, metal began to be marked with a public mark, which led to the creation of minted coins and mints.

Minted coins became popular around the 7th century BC. They were convenient to store, their weight was quite small, and it became more convenient to pay due to their exact cost.

As we see, the very creation and development of monetary units was a revolution in market relations and was simply necessary. People could create their goods faster and buy raw materials for production. We also note the evolution of the physical weight of money - from three-meter stones to paper bills. In our time, electronic currency has appeared, and now money has come to where it came from - from the minds of people.

Time Value of Money

During the existence of money, people have formed many concepts and theories about it. One of the concepts was proposed back in 1202 by the famous mathematician Fibonacci. He formulated the golden rule of business: " The amount received today is greater than the same amount received tomorrow. "

We know all this now. The value of today's money is higher than the value of the same amount received in the future and even tomorrow. This is why (though not only) banks require interest on their loans.

From all of the above, two extremely important consequences emerge that any person seeking to become more financially literate needs to understand:

- It is always worth considering the time factor when conducting financial transactions.
- Summing up monetary values relating to different periods is incorrect.

To understand what the value of money is over time, you need to calculate the value of money. This is why discounting was invented.

"Discounting is an assessment of the value of a future stream of payments based on the different values of money received at different points in time ("Fundamentals of Stochastic Financial Mathematics", Shiryaev A. N.)"

That is, simply put, discounting will help you find out what the difference is between your profit of 100 monetary units in a year and today. Please also keep in mind that it's not just about inflation, but also that if you receive 100 monetary units today, you can invest them and receive additional income, even taking into account the loss of value of the amount over time. Calculating discounted value is important, for example, for investors who want to understand whether their profits will depreciate so much that it is easier to invest the money in something more profitable and not so long-term. You become poorer if you receive the same salary for months or years and spend it on your daily needs.

What does the discount rate depend on? There are five main factors:

1. Profitability of alternative investments.
2. Cost of credit funds.
3. Inflation.
4. The period within which you expect to receive future income.
5. The risk associated with this future income

For this reason, investments are a good way to save and increase your capital. Investing money in a bank allows you, in fact, only to save your money. It is also possible to increase your capital by putting money in a bank, but this becomes possible only in the case of long-term and compound interest. But remember that in this case there is a serious risk that the bank will go bankrupt and you will lose the entire amount. And at best, you will return only part of it.

Compound interest is a good way to earn income because interest also accrues on interest. There are known cases when relatives became millionaires only because their ancestors invested a small amount of money into the account, and a century later the agreement was discovered. Of course, the bank had to pay a huge amount, but it received publicity for its longevity and attitude towards customers.

We will not give complex discounting formulas here, but we will give a simple example. Let's say in one year you expect a profit of 121 monetary units at a discount rate of 10%. Then the value of your future 121 units will be equal to 110 units: 121/(1+0.1). If in two years, then 100: 121/(1+0.1) 2. This is the time value of your money.

As we wrote above, the cost of money is also affected by inflation. Let's take a closer look at it.

Inflation

There are many different definitions of this term, so we tried to give the simplest, most accurate, and understandable one.

"Inflation is the depreciation of money, as a result of which the prices of goods and services may remain at the same level, but the goods and services themselves become less affordable."

Inflation should not be confused with rising prices, because in the second case, prices for certain groups of goods increase, but in the case of inflation, money depreciates and all goods become more expensive. When they say that the purchasing power of the population has decreased, they usually mean inflation. The depreciation of money and a general increase in prices are its main signs.

There are two exceptional cases in world history of sharp increases in prices and inflation. The uniqueness is that, in theory, the financial security of citizens should have increased:

After the discovery of America, European countries began to receive a lot of gold and silver from Peru and Mexico. This led to an increase in prices by 2.5-4 times.

In the 1840s, the development of California gold mines began, as well as mines in Australia. Gold production has increased 6 times, but prices around the world have increased by 25-50%.

The point is that a large increase in money in the economy causes prices to rise. The more money there is in the economy, the more the product depreciates. Accordingly, an increase in production could help contain inflation in these two cases, but in the first case, in the absence of industrialization and industry, this could not be done, while the second became less catastrophic precisely because of the increase in production.

What are the causes of inflation? There are six main reasons, but besides them, there are dozens and even hundreds of others that economists are still arguing about:

✔ **Money issue** Government spending increases, resulting in a decision to print more money. Emission is the release of new money.

✔ **Mass lending** In this case, finances are taken not even from savings, but from the issue of currency not backed by goods. Those. the second reason is often adjacent to the first.

✔ **Excessive taxation** Not only are fewer goods produced in this case, but the tax itself falls on the shoulders of the ordinary consumer.

✔ **Monopolization of markets and monopoly pricing** Large firms determine the price and their production costs.

✔ **Decrease in national production** This means that the previous volume of money supply corresponds to fewer goods.

✔ **Trade union monopoly** In this case, employee salaries are increased regardless of economic reasons.

As we see, with proper government management, high inflation can be avoided. Now there is only one country in the world that periodically experiences an increase in the value of money. This is the so-called deflation, and it has been characteristic of Japan in recent years.

Types of Inflation

There is an open and hidden nature of inflation. With the open, everything is simple - it is a rise in prices and a decrease in purchasing power. It is visible, and you don't need to be an economist to recognize it. Hidden inflation is much more complex and interesting. For example, in the USSR for some time there was an increase in wages and a decrease in food prices. However, the natural consequence of such suppressed inflation was a commodity shortage and huge queues.

There are also types of inflation such as:

Demand inflation is when there are fewer goods than people need.

Cost-push inflation – prices increase due to rising production costs in the face of unused resources. Thus, raw materials and resources are held up in warehouses, increasing the unit price.

Projected inflation – it can be predicted because many economic entities often behave in the same way. As mentioned above, by the end of the year the level of consumption usually increases, companies increase production, and therefore it is at this time that the inflation rate rises.

Unpredictable inflation - in this case, the rise in inflation comes as a surprise to the population and government due to the complexity of the economic system.

Balanced inflation – the prices of all goods rise almost equally. If inflation is inevitable, it is more suitable for the country's economy; the economy is not shocked by surprises.

Unbalanced inflation - in this case, the prices of some goods rise more than others. This leads to many sad consequences.

Adapted consumer expectations – information about future inflation is disseminated in society, which changes consumer psychology; demand for goods increases, which leads to higher prices.

Government intervention to suppress inflation does not always help. When the state prohibits increasing prices for a specific product, this leads to a decrease in the production of this product with all the ensuing consequences, for example, cheaper production costs and the emergence of counterfeits.

There are types of inflation depending on the growth rate:

Creeping inflation is characterized by price increases of less than 10% per year. Some Western economists consider this a completely normal process. For example, if such inflation is caused by an increase in the money supply, then eventually this money will be used, and the rate of production will also increase. But, of course, this is in theory. In practice, everything depends entirely on the adequacy of the country's leaders. In this case, such inflation gets out of control and turns into two other types described below.

Galloping inflation is characterized by rising prices from 10 to 50%. The economy is out of control and requires urgent, perhaps even unpopular, measures. State intervention is acceptable.

Hyperinflation is characterized by an increase in prices by 60%

or more and can reach astronomical numbers. We all know the example of Zimbabwe and the fact that they have a banknote of one hundred trillion Zimbabwean dollars. To cover the budget deficit, the government began to issue incredible amounts of money, which led to hyperinflation. As a result, Zimbabwe returned to barter exchange. Similar experiences also exist during the war.

The main conclusion that everyone should make for themselves is that slight inflation is a normal process, and in some cases even means economic growth. If a new money supply is poured into the country's economy, at first this leads precisely to inflation, and then the new money begins to move the economy forward, and an increase in production is observed. All this is possible only with proper management, otherwise the process will eventually get out of control.

Types of money

Over its long history, humanity has used a large number of different types of money. Initially, the material from which money was made was very important. They had to have the following properties:

Divisibility and integrability They must have the property of exchange, and also not change their value when combined.

Qualitative uniformity. Individual copies of the same denomination should not have greater value.

Portability. Low weight and volume and at the same time high cost. Those. these should not be three-meter stones with a hole in the middle. The world is striving for credit cards and electronic money with all their advantages and disadvantages.

Storability. When stored for a long time, money should not physically deteriorate or change its chemical properties.

Recognition. Money could be easily identified and its denomination understood.

Safety. There must be protection against counterfeiting and theft.

With all of the above, the type of money changed significantly and was refined, because ideally, money should have all these properties.

Commodity money

It is a product that has generally accepted value and utility. The main feature of such money is that it can be used not only as payment for goods. For example, a gold coin is valuable in itself and can be melted down and made into jewelry.

Therefore, at the dawn of economic development, the role of money was played by independent goods that would be useful to any person in any case: furs, pearls, livestock, grain, Cowrie shells, as well as bronze, copper, platinum, gold and silver coins. In Scotland, at one time, workers were paid with nails, and in Sudan, with spearheads and shovels. In prisons, cigarettes are the money.

Commodity money did not take root because it did not meet the same properties of ideal money - it was not portable, deteriorated during storage, and was difficult to divide and create. Therefore, over time, people began to invent money that was easy, quick, and cheap to make.

Secured money

At their core, they are representatives of commodity money. You could receive signs or certificates and use them to exchange them for a certain amount of goods or commodity money. For example, in Ancient Sumer you could present figurines of baked clay sheep and goats and get live goats and sheep for them. Initially, even banknotes were considered backed by money, but then this function disappeared.

Fiat money

This is the same money that we currently use. They do not have independent value but act as money because the state has laws to consider them as such. Today there are three forms of such money: banknotes, non-cash money held in a bank, and electronic money. Non-cash payments should not be confused with electronic ones, although they can eventually be deposited into a bank account. And banknotes are gradually being forced out of circulation.

Electronic money

They are used to pay for goods and services online and have the same value as real money. The development of this type of money became possible for many reasons, but the two main ones are earnings on the Internet by individuals and financial transactions between companies.

Electronic money has all the properties given earlier, but also has additional ones: they can be quickly counted, transferred, and divided. You can also pay your bills automatically, and you don't even need to spend extra time to do this. And since they do not exist in physical form, they cannot deteriorate and do not lose their qualities over time.

Cryptocurrency

The most controversial currency, about which controversy continues. Also, few people understand how it works and whether such money has a future. Let's talk specifically about Bitcoin, which is the most popular cryptocurrency.

A person does not pay a commission for transferring Bitcoin, i.e. There are no intermediaries in principle. Almost complete anonymity is guaranteed, which, of course, can become (and has already become) a field of activity for various criminal transactions. In the Bitcoin system, no person manages it; all participants in the process are equal.

Bitcoin is also inherently an indicator of the level of trust in conspiracy theories. Cryptocurrencies in their advertising focus on Big Brother, who is constantly watching us, and if we do not get out of his control, humanity will face financial slavery. To put it simply, with the mass adoption of Bitcoin, the world's banking system will likely collapse or, at a minimum, it will accept the rules of the game and change greatly. No one can say what will happen to the world economy if cryptocurrency wins. This is why cryptocurrency is so controversial.

4

Financial Planning and Accounting

Financial literacy involves not only knowledge of the theory of money and its depreciation. Any person or organization simply needs financial planning and accounting of their finances. Why is this so important? It's about the psychology of money. If you don't keep track of the money you spend and don't plan for the future, you will always spend as much as you earn. You've probably seen this yourself. Even if you managed to set aside a certain amount of money, sooner or later it is taken out of reserves and spent on current needs.

When you see with your own eyes the amount of money earned and spent, you avoid the temptation to spend all your earnings, begin to save part of your salary and think about investments. Therefore, financial planning does a very important job - it clearly shows all your transactions with money. Those who find this activity boring and don't plan it always wonder where all the money disappears and why they constantly lack it.

Even if at some point their income doubles, they end up with the same problem of not having enough money after some time because they have no financial goal. And if a person takes out a loan, the situation worsens for a very long time. Now you understand how important financial accounting is, so let's get down to this topic in more detail.

It's worth saying right away that if you think that the essence of planning is to save money and buy a car or a house, this is the main mistake that you will need to correct. You'll see why this kind of thinking is economically wrong in Lesson Four. But before that, you must realize equally important things.

Before we begin personal financial planning, let's consider organizational planning. If you want to open your own business in the future, you will need financial planning.

Financial planning of the organization

Financial planning is the planning of all income and expenses to ensure the development of the organization ("Financial management and taxation of organizations", Levchaev A.P.) There can be several financial plans depending on the goals and directions. Such a plan is a balance sheet form in the form of grouped items of income and expenses planned to be received and financed in the coming period.

Before you begin developing a financial plan, you need to understand the objectives of financial planning.

The main objectives of financial planning are:

1. Determining ways to effectively invest capital.
2. Control over financial condition.

3. Respect for the interests of investors and shareholders.
4. Establishing reasonable relations with the budget, banks and extra-budgetary funds.
5. Identification of hidden reserves.
6. Providing the necessary resources for the organization's activities.

Before you start drawing up a plan, you need to understand the financial condition of the organization. To treat a patient and maintain his health, he needs to be diagnosed. This is exactly what should be done first.

The budget can be at the level of personal finance, organization or state. Despite the different scales, the budget of any level has the same features and criteria. For example, if your or the government's revenues exceed expenses, it is called a budget surplus. If the number of expenses exceeds income, then a budget deficit arises and things begin to get out of control. A surplus is more desirable than a deficit, but excess money must be put into circulation immediately, maintaining balance.

At first, you may think that a budget and a financial plan are one and the same thing. The only difference can be that the financial plan is sometimes supplemented with some recommendations and goals, while the budget mainly deals with numbers and graphs. The financial plan includes a budget, and you can often put an equal sign between them.

In addition to the tasks of financial planning, there are also its principles:

✔ **Forecasting** . The economic state of the organization and the country (sometimes the whole world, if it is a transnational corporation) is analyzed. The quality of the forecast determines the quality of the financial plan.

✔ **Optimization** . This means reducing costs without harming the organization and its employees and the most effective investment of money.

✔ **Control** . A sound financial plan prevents irresponsibility, clearly shows who is responsible for what, and allows you to control all aspects of the organization.

✔ **Documentation** . Record keeping is a natural consequence of control.

✔ **Coordination** . Financial plans of different departments should be developed in close connection with each other. Sometimes it makes sense to focus (read: invest more money) in one department while sacrificing some spending on another.

✔ **Prioritization** . In order to fulfill the financial plan, the manager must define clear and concise goals . All actions and financial transactions of the organization must be subject to the main priorities. Without priorities, a company can spend a lot of money on completely unnecessary areas and simply suffer financial collapse.

✔ **Adequacy** . It is very commendable to set ambitious goals for yourself, but unsupported ambitions can lead to dire consequences.

✔ **Versatility and flexibility** . The plan may be adjusted to suit the economic climate. The economy changes every day, so you need to monitor its trends and make adjustments to your financial plan.

Creating a financial plan is a complex and complex undertaking. Therefore, we will focus on common and understandable features. Income and expenses form the basis of the budget of any organization, state or ordinary person.

Income and funds received:

- Profit from the sale of products, works and services.
- Profit from other sales (fixed assets and other assets).
- Depreciation deductions.
- Receipt of money from other companies.
- Planned income that is not related to the sale of goods, works and services. This could be income from securities, equity participation in the authorized capital of other companies, leasing of property, or storing finances on deposits.

Expenses and deductions:

- Taxes paid from profits, and others.
- Depreciation expenses.
- Wage.
- Cost of raw materials and other resources.
- Loan repayments.
- Rental of premises.
- Other expenses.

This is all that any financially literate person needs to know if they are not yet considering running their own organization. When you firmly decide to take this path, you will have to study a lot more information or hire a financial advisor.

Now it's time to look at personal financial planning, which you can master yourself by following certain instructions.

Personal financial planning

Before you move on to the topic of the lesson, we suggest you solve a small case to check how carefully you approach personal finance planning.

For competent personal financial planning, it won't hurt you to take a course on time management . This course will teach you how to properly allocate time in different areas to generate income from them. In the fourth lesson, we will look at ways to earn additional income, so you need to learn how to set the right goals and develop a strategy for achieving them, properly distributing your time and effort. Combining these two skills will help you get on your feet financially.

First of all, you need to realize the fact that any saved monetary unit can turn, after some time, into two or more. If it is spent on something unnecessary, you lose this opportunity. Remember how many useless expenses you made in a year, and multiply this figure by three - you could probably get the same amount in a year or two with the right investments.

This is why most financially successful people reached their peaks - they are used to spending the minimum and investing the rest of the money in something. After all, everyone knows the stories when those who won the lottery eventually became beggars again in just a year. They were not financially literate. However, if they spent at least a couple of hours on financial planning, they could clearly see that after just a year this money would not be left.

Before you create your personal financial plan, you should know the principles of personal finance planning:

The principle of economy. Patience is strength. This quality helps any person in any area of life, and it will also help in personal finance. The desire for immediate gratification and impatience are signs of immature, childish behavior. We all know that we need to save, but a very small percentage of people do it. However, you shouldn't go to extremes, because saving for the sake of saving won't lead to any good either. Later we will tell you what to do with the money you save.

The principle of sufficiency. We need to put a barrier between ourselves and modern media. The function of any advertisement is to show you that you will be unhappy if you do not buy some product. Learn to think about the usefulness of purchasing a product from a value perspective. If a product will bring you nothing but dubious pleasure, do not buy it. Be happy with your current situation and think that a sense of self-sufficiency will help you make it even better. Self-sufficiency does not mean sitting back, it means being happy now, but at the same time knowing how you can become even better. Be grateful - this is one of the most underrated qualities in a person.

Operating principle. For a good life, it is very important to find a job where you do not think only about money. In this case, your productivity will increase several times, and with it your income. Love what you do. This will help you always be in high spirits and find time and energy for much more.

Research principle. Financial literacy presupposes a constant conscious attitude towards money and opportunities. Find out which products and products you actually need and don't overpay for more expensive versions. All of your financial decisions today affect you and your family in the future.

The principle of priority. Every day we are faced with one very important problem - what to spend and where to invest our money. Even millionaires face this. Remember that if you buy one expensive item, you are deprived of another. With the help of one product or service you become smarter and better, with the help of the second you degrade. As practice shows, the second products are purchased much more often. Distinguish the first from the second.

Tracking principle . Money management should become a habit. Thoughtless spending of money leads to financial ruin. Track and always be aware of how much money you have and what you spend it on.

The principle of frugal living . Even if only for a while. You need to ensure that your income is generated without your participation, and only then will you be able to afford much more. If your passive income reaches the amount you need and makes you happy non-stop, this is a sure sign that you have achieved financial independence. A modest life does not mean a bad life, it means a more reasonable one. Of course, if you work with people, you should have nice and neat clothes. The point is to avoid buying unnecessary clothes.

The principle of avoiding debt . Any loan or debt eats up part of your financial future. It is possible in some cases, which we will talk about later.

The principle of investing . Remember inflation? Simply storing money is, of course, better than spending it thoughtlessly, but such behavior cannot be called effective either. Investing always carries a certain risk, but you cannot live without it in the world of money. Read a lot of books, watch videos and think.

The principle of caution . A wealthy person is not characterized by an expensive car, but by how many months he can live if he loses his job today. They say that if you have enough money to live a good life for six months, then you can be considered middle class. And yet, the essence of financial well-being is not to work (or work where you like) and at the same time have a constant flow of income.

The principle of cooperation . Of course, you can make a good income working alone, but the information age offers many opportunities for cooperation with other people. The principle of synergy works very well in the financial sector. With the right team, anyone can generate more income.

Now that we have become familiar with the principles of personal finance planning, it's time to move on to practice.

Five Steps to Financial Planning

Financial planning takes into account only five steps . Each step should be treated with due attention and not proceed to the next one until you have finally dealt with the previous one.

Grade

First of all, you need to clearly assess what your assets and liabilities are. First, determine how much cash and electronic money you have. Then write down in the "assets" column what brings you income: deposit, monthly salary, investments. In the "liabilities" column, write down everything that does not bring you money and takes money out of you: car, house or mortgage, loan, rent bills, Internet and mobile phone use. Determine at least the approximate amount of money you spend per month on food, clothing and entertainment. And yes, the car and apartment are your liabilities, and we will talk about this separately.

Get rid of loans. You must understand that in the end you will still give it away, but it will extract interest from you and create a debtor syndrome. Remember: no debt, minimal needs can be met with any income. Of course, there is no need to go to extremes - living in a car or walking around in torn clothes.

Simply put, you should end up seeing two approximate figures: your total income and expenses per month.

Target

You can't go anywhere without a goal, especially if it's long-term. Almost everyone is capable of collecting a certain amount in a couple of months, but if we are talking about several years, then you need iron discipline and motivation . And it is goal setting that will help you with this.

Ideally, you should plan several years in advance because this is what constitutes financially savvy behavior. For example, this could be the entry "A million dollars in ten years." It has its drawbacks, but it's better than nothing. Of course, your goal should be objective, but on the other hand, it is very easy to underestimate yourself, and in the end you will get less than you could. When you start to understand your finances and invest money, you will realize that anyone on the planet can save a million dollars. Let's think about what goal a financially literate person should set for himself.

Your financial goal should not be something like "Buy a car in two years" or "Buy a house in five years." This is economically incorrect thinking because even if you eventually achieve this, your expenses will increase a lot and you will spend the rest of your life keeping your car or home running. A goal of "Have a million dollars in ten years" is better, but it means that after that period of time you will simply start spending your million and end up back where you started financially. Your goal should be to create passive sources of income. Roughly speaking, this could be a million-dollar bank account that will allow you not to work and withdraw good interest every year. However, banks and the economic situation are unstable, so you need to remember another golden rule: don't put all your eggs in one basket.

If your goal is "A million dollars in the bank and five more sources of passive income from different investments," this is already close to financial solvency.

Create a plan

The first step in creating a plan is to cut your expenses. This is the cornerstone of financial literacy. Remember that a person is able to spend all the money he has, regardless of his income level. Therefore, first of all, find expense items that can be reduced or eliminated altogether.

And it is this very 50% that you should save for, if not your entire life, then at least for the duration of this financial plan. This is the second step.

Remember that if you wish and have certain skills, one monetary unit can be turned into three or more. Therefore, the more you save, the greater the chance of increasing this amount. If you don't save a penny, then through simple calculations you get zero multiplied by any number, and you end up with zero.

The third step is investing. We will talk about this separately and in great detail.

So, cut your expenses, save your money and invest. Even if you just won a million dollars in the lottery. This applies to every person, regardless of their current income level.

Execution of the plan

Hang it in a visible place. If you use an app, have it on your home screen so you can instantly go into it and make any changes. If you bought food, immediately add this amount to your expense items, while clearly understanding how much you have allocated for food per month. You can go on a diet, this is generally a great way to become healthy and rich.

Your financial plan should become your second nature. We do not advise you to think only in terms of money, because otherwise you will degrade as a person, but do not forget about your goals. The best and greatest goals are achieved through personal effectiveness and financial literacy. Remain human, but remember your financial well-being.

By the way, if you don't like the word "plan," come up with your own motivational word. Think about a word that will inspire you rather than bore you.

Monitoring and reassessment

There is no problem in adjusting the plan. When you compiled the first version, you probably still had a very vague understanding of where you would invest your money. Once you've cut your expenses and started saving, ideally half of your income, it may take a couple of months before you have a good amount accumulated there. Spend these months on your financial books and then adjust your financial plan. It should always change towards reducing costs and optimizing investments, and not vice versa. This is the main rule for adjusting your personal financial plan.

Of course, you may have allocated a completely insignificant amount of money for food, in which case you can increase your food expenses. Also, do not forget about products that tend to run out for a long time. For example, you may not think about shampoo and razor blades, but after a while you will need them. In this case, it makes sense to buy in bulk, but you should take money for these expenses only from other expenses.

At this point, you probably think that your life will turn into a living hell. This is true, but provided that you do not look for new sources of income. Agree that if you save 50% of your income for investments, new sources of income will allow you to eventually get out of the first difficulties and spend more money on entertainment and other things. Remember that there is no other way. No one forbids you to enjoy life and at the same time look for new opportunities that life offers.

As we already said, financial planning can seem like a very boring activity because most people in the world don't like numbers. But people love beautiful graphics and colorful pictures more. Let's consider mobile applications that will always be at your fingertips and have good visibility and interface.

Programs for planning a personal budget

Monefy

This shareware program has a very nice interface and has a number of advantages. For example, using synchronization with the Dropbox service, you can manage your family budget. Any entry in this application will be visible to those people with whom you maintain this budget. However, you can also use it just for yourself. The application has a built-in calculator, which is very convenient.

It is also worth noting a beautiful and informative graph that will help you see in a few seconds where you spend the most money and what brings you the most income. You can see your income and expenses by day, week, month and year, which will help you be more conscious about your money.

Money Lover

This application is not only about accounting and financial planning, it is constantly evolving and is already trying to cover many aspects of a person's life. You can create two wallets for free; for the rest you will have to pay a small amount of money.

Another good difference from other applications are the two tabs "I owe" and "I am owed". As you understand, the first tab should always be clean, and having a second tab will not always make your life better. But if this happens, the application will help you not to forget about all your debts.

There is also a "Bills" tab that allows you to finally find out the total amount of your all bills: rent, rent, Internet, phone, etc.

In addition to all this, the program contains a currency converter, interest rate calculation and is able to find the nearest ATM.

Financius

The simplest application presented. It consists of three simple menu items: "Accounts", "Transactions" and "Reports". You can track the financial status of your company or any family member. There is no financial planning here, but if you are not an experienced app user, you can start there. It's free and ad-free.

CoinKeeper

This application is about financial management and is presented in a game form. In order to spend money on something, you need to throw a coin on a specific icon. There is an interesting feature called "Automatic Budget" - it allows you to quickly calculate the main categories of expenses for the month.

You can set reminders for recurring expenses and also keep track of it with your family.

Toshl

What's unique about the app is that it constantly reminds you that you might be going over budget. However, its disadvantages are the paid use, as well as the fact that some things need to be entered manually.

We advise you to try all these apps and eventually choose the one that suits you best. They are developing and evolving, which means that other functions may be added soon. If you are unable to use mobile applications, Internet services are offered for your services. There are a large number of them, and it is quite difficult to single out any one separately.

5

Financial Analysis

The internal and external business environment is changeable, so a firm's ability to maintain its solvency and financial stability can say a lot about its prospects. Economics and business require precision in numerical terms and do not tolerate subjective and artistic descriptions.

Financial analysis was created to reveal the true state of affairs. It is impartial and clear because it deals with numbers and indicators. A financially literate person must distinguish between a profitable company and an unprofitable one if he intends to make money in business and investment.

"Financial analysis is an assessment of the economic health of any company. Financial indicators, ratios, ratings and multipliers are studied, and on their basis a conclusion is drawn about the financial condition of the organization"

Who might need financial analysis? For example, the top management of the company. Or investors who want to explore whether it's worth investing in. Even banks that decide whether to provide a loan to this organization. The company can also list its shares on the stock exchange, and this will also require understanding its financial condition.

In this chapter, we will look at situations in which a person has access to all possible company information. But not every person has access to the true state of affairs in the organization in which he wants to invest money or with which he wants to cooperate. To do this, you can use indirect sources of information. Of course, this will not always be enough, but you can draw some conclusions. We offer you tools such as:

- Exchange rates.
- State of the economy, financial sector, political and economic state.
- Securities rates, yield on securities.
- Indicators of the financial condition of other companies

This is called external data, and it can be your tool for assessing the prospects of your investments. For example, if you wanted to buy shares of a company, but you do not have access to financial statements, then the above indicators can partially help you.

Financial Analysis Tools

Cost-benefit analysis

In economic language, "profitability" is understood as "profitability", so in the future we will use this term. The profitability ratio is calculated as the ratio of profit to assets, resources and flows. Profitability ratios are often expressed as percentages.

Understand the difference between income and profit. Income is all the money you receive from your activities. Profit is a financial result. Those. if you made $500 from selling goods, that's your income. You bought these goods somewhere or made them, and they cost you $300. So your profit is $200.

There can be quite a lot of profitability indicators. Let's look at the most important of them:

Profitability of products sold This is the ratio of profit from sales to the cost of goods sold. If your profit is $1000, and the cost of the products you sold is $800, this figure is calculated as follows: (1000/800) * 100% = 125%. We hope you perform such mathematical calculations without a calculator.

Return on assets. Reflects the efficiency of using the company's assets to generate profit. Those. you can find out how effectively you are using your
   company's assets. If you made a profit of $1000 in a month, and the average value of your assets is $2000, this indicator is calculated as follows: (1000/2000)*100% = 50%.

Return on equity. This is the ratio of profit to the average amount of equity capital for the period. Let's say you earned $5,000 in a month, and you invest an average of $1,000 of home equity per month. Then you will calculate this indicator as follows: (5000/1000)*100% = 500%. A very good indicator. True, it may not be very objective and will not say anything about the state of affairs of your company if you do not calculate other indicators.

Financial stability analysis

Financial stability ratios of an enterprise are indicators that clearly demonstrate the level of stability of an enterprise in financial terms.

The financial independence ratio is a financial ratio equal to the ratio of equity capital and reserves to the total assets of the enterprise. For this purpose, the balance sheet of this organization is used. This indicator reflects the share of the organization's assets that are covered by equity capital.

This ratio is needed by banks that issue loans. The higher it is, the more likely the bank will give a loan to your company, because you will be able to pay off the debt with your assets. Remember we already said that the bank considers your liabilities as its assets? In this case, the difference is that the company's assets are simply necessary, because without most of them it simply cannot function.

The financial dependence ratio is an indicator that is the opposite of the financial independence ratio. It shows the extent to which a company depends on external sources of financing. This indicator is also necessary for banks to make decisions on issuing a loan.

Solvency and liquidity analysis

Solvency is the company's ability to timely fulfill monetary obligations stipulated by law or contract. Insolvency, on the contrary, shows the inability of a company to pay obligations to a creditor. May cause bankruptcy.

Asset (property) liquidity analysis calculates an indicator that indicates how quickly an organization's assets can be sold if it is unable to repay its loan debts.

Investment Analysis

This is a set of techniques and methods for developing and assessing the feasibility of investments in order for the investor to make an effective decision.

Based on this analysis, management decides whether the company will invest in short-term and long-term investments. Some investments are more profitable than others, so the challenge is also to find the most effective ones. Several tools are used for this: discounted payback period, net present value, internal form of return and return on investment index.

The discounted payback period (DPP) characterizes the change in the purchasing power of money, the value of which, as we remember, decreases over time. You, as an investor, need to know how long it will take to start receiving income from your investments, and bring this amount into line with the present moment. Sometimes it doesn't even make sense to invest, because it either won't pay off or will pay off minimally.

There is a tool called net present value (NPV). This is the current value of an investment project, determined by taking into account all current and future income at the appropriate interest rate. If this indicator is positive, then funds can be invested in the project.

Net present value can be used not only in investments, but also in business. Using this tool, a company can calculate the feasibility of expanding its products. Everything is exactly the same here: if this indicator is positive, then it's worth expanding products.

The third tool is called **internal rate of return (IRR)**, and it is also used both in business and in assessing the feasibility of investment projects. You can also calculate this indicator online. If you get a zero value, you will only get back your investment, but nothing more. The higher the internal rate of return, the better.

Return on investment index (PI) is an indicator of investment efficiency, representing the ratio of discounted income to the amount of investment capital. It is also sometimes called the profitability index or profitability index.

Bankruptcy probability analysis

As history shows, very often, several months before bankruptcy, no one in the company even suspects that the company will collapse. Everything seems to be going well and there is no reason to think that anything will go wrong.

What criteria are used to assess the likelihood of bankruptcy? We have already become acquainted with some indicators :

1. Current ratio.
2. Financial dependency ratio.
3. Solvency restoration coefficient.

4. Autonomy coefficient.
5. Covering fixed financial expenses.

This analysis is important for banks issuing loans. They often analyze the probability of bankruptcy and issue or not issue a loan depending on the results. Also, such indicators are important for shareholders, investors and partners of this company, because they must understand that they are investing money in a promising enterprise. Of course, they must look for this information themselves, because the company itself will hide it or block access to it.

Business market value analysis

This may be useful for those who want to buy an existing business. A businessman hires a financial analyst who makes all the calculations: the recommended value of the business and the potential income of the enterprise after a certain period of time. If an investor hires a financial analyst, then, first of all, it is important for him to understand one simple thing - whether the indicated value corresponds to his investment interests.

This is a very difficult job. The average business market value analysis report is approximately 300 pages.

There are three approaches to assessing the value of a business : income, expense and comparative. By the way, it is also used before purchasing real estate.

The essence of the expense approach is that all assets of the enterprise (buildings, machinery, equipment, etc.) are first assessed and summed up, and then liabilities are subtracted from this amount. The resulting figure shows the value of the enterprise's equity capital.

The comparative (market) approach is based on the principle of substitution. Competing organizations are selected for comparison. Usually, with this approach, it is difficult to compare two companies due to some differences, so it is necessary to adjust the data. All possible information about the company that can be purchased is collected and compared with a similar organization.

The comparative approach uses methods of the capital market, transactions, industry coefficients (market multiplier):

The capital market method is focused on assessing the enterprise as an operating one, which expects to continue to function. It is based on stock market prices.

The transaction method is used when the investor intends to close the enterprise or significantly reduce production volumes. Therefore, this method is based on precedent - cases of sale of similar enterprises.

The market multiplier method is focused on assessing the enterprise as an operating one that will continue to function. The most commonly used valuation multiples are price/gross earnings, price/net earnings, and price/cash flow.

All three approaches are interconnected because none of them separately can serve as an objective factor. Therefore, it is recommended to use all approaches. Some companies provide business valuation services, but these services are quite expensive.

Break Even

Break-even point (BEP) is the volume of production and sales of products at which costs will be offset by income, and with the production and sale of each subsequent unit of product the enterprise begins to make a profit. It is also sometimes called the critical point or CVP point.

The break-even point is calculated in units of production, in monetary terms or taking into account the expected profit margin.

The break-even point in monetary terms is the minimum amount of income at which costs are fully recouped.

BEP TFC/(C/P), where TFC is the value of fixed costs, P is the cost of a unit of production (sales), C is the profit per unit of production without taking into account fixed costs.

The break-even point in units of production is the minimum quantity of product at which the income from the sale of this product completely covers all the costs of its production.

BEP TFC/C TFC/(P-AVC), where AVC is the value of variable costs per unit of production.

Stock Exchanges

We simply cannot ignore the stock exchange and some indicators related to the global economy.

"A stock exchange is a financial institution that ensures the regular

functioning of the securities market. Some stock exchanges are real places (for example, the New York Stock Exchange), while others are purely virtual (for example, NASDAQ)"

Why would any company list its shares on the stock exchange? There are many reasons, but the main one is that this will allow the company to make a large profit from the shares sold. The downside is that such a company partially loses its independence. For example, Sergey Brin and Larry Page delayed the placement of Google shares on the stock exchange until the last minute and used various strategic tricks. By law, they were forced to do this, so Page and Brin found a way out: the shares had two classes: A and B. The first was privileged and intended only for company employees, while the second class was somewhat limited and was sold to anyone.

However, there are also those who became billionaires by playing on the stock exchange. It could be a genius like Buffett or just a random investor who got incredibly lucky. Some people use inside information. For example, when shares are listed on the stock exchange by a successful company, the prices per share are quite high. Let's assume that this company wants to change management soon - then the share price would go down. However, the head of the company does not talk about this publicly, and may also not talk about significant problems of the company. This alone is a criminal offense, and if such information is transmitted to a large future shareholder (who wants to speculate on these shares), punishment may await him too. Withholding information is a form of lying .

The ten largest financial exchanges in the world:

NYSE Euronext This is a group of companies formed as a result of the merger of the world's largest New York Stock Exchange (NYSE) and the European exchange Euronext.

NASDAQ This exchange specializes in shares of high-tech companies. It lists shares of 3,200 companies.

Tokyo Stock Exchange The exchange is a member of the Federation of Stock Exchanges of Asia and Oceania. The value of all securities traded on the Tokyo Stock Exchange exceeds $5 trillion.

London Stock Exchange It was officially founded in 1801, but its history actually began in 1570, when the Royal Exchange was built. In order for a company to list its shares on this exchange, it needs to meet several conditions: have a market capitalization of at least 700 thousand pounds sterling and disclose financial, commercial and management information.

Shanghai Stock Exchange The stock market capitalization is $286 billion, and the number of companies that have placed their shares exceeds 800.

Hong Kong Stock Exchange Has a capitalization of 3 trillion US dollars.

Toronto Stock Exchange Capitalization volume is 1.6 trillion dollars.

Bombay Stock Exchange It has a capitalization of $1 trillion, and the number of companies that have placed their shares is about 5 thousand.

National Stock Exchange of India Second Stock Exchange of India.

Sao Paulo Stock Exchange Largest stock exchange in Latin America.

As you can see, stock exchanges, as a rule, are developed in those countries that themselves have powerful economies. India's dual presence on this list may be a little surprising, but it's not news to people interested in economics.

Dow Jones Industrial Average

It's time to get acquainted with the Dow Jones Industrial Average. You will understand how simple it is, what it means and how to interpret it.

The Dow Jones Industrial Average covers the 30 largest companies in America. The prefix "industrial" is a nod to history because many of the companies included in the index are currently not in that industry. Now, when calculating the index, a scaled average is used - the sum of prices is divided by a certain divisor, which is constantly changing. With some adjustments, we can say that this index is the arithmetic average of the stock prices of 30 American companies.

You may ask, what does the Dow Jones Industrial Average have to do with financial analysis? The fact is that this index is unofficially called an indicator of the state of the economy of the United States and the whole world. Of course, this is an indirect indicator, but a very eloquent one. If the top 30 US companies are in crisis, then so is the entire economy. The higher the index, the better the state of the economy.

The historical maximum was reached relatively recently – on May 19, 2015.

We will not give the names of all thirty companies; we will give only the ten most interesting and familiar to everyone.

Ten companies included in the Dow Jones Industrial Average:

Apple. The company entered the index only in 2015.
   Coca-Cola. Entered the index in 1987.

Microsoft. Entered the index in 1999.
Visa. Entered the index in 2013.
Wal-Mart. Entered the index in 1997.
Walt Disney. Entered the index in 1991.
Procter & Gamble. Entered the index in 1932.
McDonald's. Entered the index in 1985.
Nike. Entered the index in 2013.
Intel. Entered the index in 1999.

Companies are constantly pushing each other out of this list. For example, in 2015, Apple ousted the largest telecommunications corporation AT&T.

Some economists believe that the best indicator of the American economy is the S&P 500. This is a stock index whose basket includes 500 selected US public companies.

Both indices are popular and represent a barometer of the American economy. Now you are armed with this tool too.

6

Investing and Saving

We are moving on to a very interesting section of financial literacy. Like the previous ones, this lesson invites you to learn a simple sequence of actions that... It's quite possible that in just a couple of years they can make you a wealthy person.

In the introductory chapter, we already told you that you can become a millionaire without investing (such are, for example, actors and athletes), but these people, as a rule, do not have financial literacy, and end up losing all their money. This is all because they do not know or do not want to know the two rules that we will talk about now..

Without investing and saving, it is almost impossible to become a wealthy person for life. Even if you have a lot of money, this does not guarantee you a comfortable future. That's why two rules are so important: accumulate and invest.

What is accumulation? Saving is setting aside part of your income. This alone is better than buying unnecessary things. If you save a third or half of your income, look for new sources and increase your capital, after a short period of time (three to six months) you can start investing.

However, accumulation is, in fact, a lifelong process and there is nothing wrong with it. Even when you become successful at investing, you should still save in order to have a more substantial amount for serious investments. When you stop saving, your financial viability, and with it your income, drops. So this is the first and very simple rule : from today until the end of your life, accumulate your financial resources.

This doesn't mean you can't afford a nice car or house. You can, but not if it's all your money. Many rich people believe that you can only afford a $200,000 house when you have $1.5 million, half of which is in your extra income. Otherwise, you will have to work your whole life to pay the bills for this one.

Saving is a three-step process: cutting down unnecessary expenses, saving money from all your income, and preparing to invest.

Therefore, our second rule is: invest.

Investing is investing capital with the aim of making a profit. An investor can be called a person who invests money in something, watches his income grow, and at the same time, in fact, does nothing else. Investing is preceded by serious work of analysis.

Investment theory is incomplete without the cash flow quadrant. The famous entrepreneur and writer Robert Kiyosaki clearly showed that any person works in one of the four sectors of this quadrant. Each sector is very different from the other. Kiyosaki says that every quadrant has its advantages and disadvantages, but he still recommends that every person be on the right side of the quadrant.

Cash Flow Quadrant

Kiyosaki divides the quadrant into two sides: left and right. Let's look at each sector separately:

Left side: workers. They trade their time for money. Workers usually have a fixed wage and some government guarantees. Such people believe that they are safe, because they have a stable salary, and when they grow old, they will have a pension. However, this is actually the most dangerous sector. These people usually do not save any money, and if there is a big crisis in the country or in the world, they lose everything and even more - their houses and cars.

Left side: self-employed. These could be freelancers, small businessmen, bloggers, and even dentists who have started their own business. These people also trade their time for money. They are their own bosses because they don't like to be bossed around. However, they spend all their time on their business and have practically no free time due to the fact that no one else will do their work except them. In this sector, as a rule, there is more income than that of workers, but still not enough for a prosperous and quiet life.

Right side: big businessmen. These are already quite wealthy people, and some of them can afford to temporarily retire from business, traveling and doing what they love. They have people who can do all the work, but they need to look after their company and do long-term planning. However, you may not work in this sector and focus on the most profitable and main sector, which will be discussed below.

Right side: investors. This is exactly the sector that every person should ideally strive for. In addition to the fact that investors are wealthy people, they are also the most protected from all possible crises. They own a wide variety of assets, and even if a global crisis occurs, they do not go bankrupt, and some even become even richer. As a rule, investors cooperate with large businessmen. They invest their money in big businesses and just wait for their profits. Also, investors play in the stock market and very often win because they know much more than ordinary people.

Almost every millionaire was in one of four quadrants. He could start his journey as a simple bank clerk, then try to work for himself, create his own large company and eventually become an investor. Some millionaires skipped one of the left sectors. And the smallest part started immediately from the right side. So if you're currently on the left side, it doesn't mean you're doomed. Many people went through this and became incredibly wealthy people. This is a normal process.

Investors generate the best possible income - passive or residual income.

Your goal is to ensure that your assets begin to generate passive income, and preferably more than you need (so that you can continue to save). It is at this stage that you can buy yourself a house, a car and other benefits that suck money out of you. Now you can afford it and not be afraid that these benefits will disappear.

Investing requires diversification . This is another golden rule for any businessman and investor: don't put all your eggs in one basket. The external environment and the economy are changing, and due to repeating cycles, you cannot be sure that any one area will prosper for decades. When we talk further about ways to make extra money and investments, you should understand that it is extremely important to generate income and invest money in several different areas.

Diversification is a very logical and correct tool. If one investment brings you a 25% return per year and that's where almost all of your money is, your responsibility is to find two or three more sources of passive income with (ideally) the same percentage of return. This way you minimize your risks and losses. Investors generally love to say these last two words. For them this is not an empty phrase. Two more words they love are profit and term. Any investor, before investing his money, should know what profit and for how long he will receive, as well as what risks and losses there are. Only after this is a decision made on the feasibility of the investment. Diversification insures them in case of crisis and collapse of one area.

Before we begin to study sources of passive income, let's pay attention to credit and see if it is so unambiguously bad.

Credit as an ambiguous income generator

Credit is a misunderstood and undervalued tool in financial relationships. Skillful handling of credit distinguishes a financially literate person from an illiterate one. An illiterate person uses credit to trap himself in a vicious financial circle, i.e. into poverty or the rat race (according to Kiyosaki). A competent person uses a loan to his advantage, with the help of it he earns new money.

Buying a car or apartment on credit is the most controversial transaction, while investing credit money in investments or business is considered the right, albeit risky, step.

Robert Kiyosaki calls buying a house or car a liability. In this case, the word "liability" does not have a canonical financial meaning; it refers to a certain product you buy that does not make new money. Buying a car and home with cash or credit is a liability because you lose your own money and have to pay interest. According to various estimates, when buying a car, you lose from 10 to 20% of its value after leaving the dealership

Banks call your car an asset and they are right. But this is their asset. For you, the car is a liability, because it sucks your money. Gasoline, insurance, winter tires, technical inspection and repairs, possible minor accidents - write down all these expenses on paper and calculate how much it will cost you in one year. If you buy a car on credit, the situation gets even worse.

Many people believe that nowadays it is much more profitable to use taxi services. Not only do you save money and get rid of headaches due to possible accidents, but you also don't waste your time on repairing and washing your car. You don't wake up at night because the alarm is blaring in the yard. However, when you become a wealthy person, you will be able to afford a car, but only from passive income.

In addition, you can take money to start your own business . This is a riskier venture, because it is one thing to work as a designer and quite another as a businessman. However, of course it's up to you to decide.

We cannot help but touch upon the topic of the financial stability of the state when it comes to loans.

When interest rates are low, the number of debtors increases; when interest rates are high, it decreases. If we talk about the country's economy as a whole, it grows along with the increase in debtors, because this allows financial flows to move through the financial system, like blood in the circulatory system.

Spending stimulates the economy, which is why the credit system is so important for any country. The consumer society is mercilessly criticized in our time, however, if you think carefully, it is this process that gives impetus to the development of the economy, and nothing better has yet been invented. One person's expenses are another's income. No spending - no income. If everyone abruptly listens to the critics of the consumer society, this will lead to catastrophic consequences.

That is, on the one hand, when you buy a car, you get new expenses for yourself, and on the other hand, you move the economy of your country forward, because someone creates these cars as well as parts for them. This means that people working in production plants receive salaries and bonuses. This is why many people have such ambivalent attitudes towards consumer society: it has its advantages for society, but at the same time its disadvantages for the individual.

Since our course is called "Financial Literacy", we do not recommend that you buy anything that will not bring you additional income. But we couldn't help but tell you that this situation has a downside. There are many contradictory and confusing things in economics.

Let's try to consolidate what was said above.

Assets and liabilities

An asset is anything that brings you income. These are all your good investments, shares, business, website, renting out an apartment or house. Precious metals can also be assets, but they have a significant drawback - extremely low liquidity. Those. It is quite possible that it will take you several weeks to sell the precious metal at a profit. Pawn shops are filled with such illiquid goods simply because a person needs money here and now. Therefore, he is forced to sell at a loss. However, precious metals increase in value every year.

A liability is everything that does not bring you income or also requires expenses. This is a car, a new big house, interest on an inappropriate loan, as well as any thing you bought that is not generating income. When an investor or economist teaches you that a car is your asset (and you are not a professional driver or a taxi driver), turn around and walk away. Because in reality he is a banker or thinks like a banker.

Get rid of liabilities and create assets. This is a very simple rule.

Finally, it's time to take a closer look at investments. In this lesson about investing, we simply cannot ignore the advice of one of the best investors in the world, Warren Buffett.

Warren Buffett's investing rules

Never confuse price and value

This is the most important rule of a good investor, while a businessman and trader can swap these two things in the client's mind.

You, as a future investor, are simply obliged to look for a product whose value is higher than its price. This is the cornerstone of any investment mindset. Of course, if you buy an item at a price above its value, you may end up selling it for a higher price. However, in this course we are talking about how to become an investor, not a trader.

People lose millions and sometimes their lives without understanding the difference between price and value. Ask yourself questions: "How much should I really pay for this business?", "What is the value of this thing and is it less than its price?", "Is a share of this company worth more than its real value?" . It is extremely difficult to calculate the true value of any asset, but you should at least clearly understand that its price is adequate to its value. Businessmen who buy and sell real estate know the difference between price and value and use it very wisely.

Let's take a break from investing for a second and take a simple example - a book. One book worth two kilograms of oranges can change your life so much that after some time you will become a successful person. In this case, the value of the book is a thousand times higher than its price. Therefore, when investing in business and stocks, do not forget about the main object that needs investment - your brain .

Leave the game on time
Buffett says that trouble does not come alone. If you have invested money in a business and there are only losses from it, feel free to sell it and do not regret the losses, otherwise you will lose even more. Many financially illiterate people continue to scrape water out of a leaky boat and end up losing even more.

Loss aversion is a well-known psychological phenomenon that relates to all areas of life. A person will finish watching a terribly boring movie only because he has already spent an hour watching it. Likewise, a bad investor will invest more and more money because he really regrets the money he has already lost.

Stocks are better than bonds over the long term
We will talk in more detail about the stock exchange and shares in the

next lesson, and here we will give the meanings of shares and bonds.

A bond is a loan, and in this case you are the bank. You can lend a certain amount of money to a commercial or government organization at interest and receive a bond, which will be your security. At the same time, you agree with the organization on how long the repayment will last. During this period, you will earn interest, and when it expires, the company will give you the amount you lent to it.

A share is a security that gives its owner the right to receive part of the company's profits, as well as sometimes participate in its management.

It's all about risks. Bonds are safer and slower in generating income, while holding stocks for the long term can make a person incredibly rich. Or maybe it won't make you rich. If the company goes bankrupt, the investor will lose all the money invested in the stock. Therefore, you need to choose a company wisely, and also learn to understand the laws of economics, business and the securities market.

In this case, Buffett is diversifying - he buys shares of a large number of companies, and many of them generate huge profits in 10-15 years.

Stock volatility does not mean risk

Volatility is a measure of the variability of a stock's price, i.e. maximum and minimum values.

Buffett points out that when a person becomes the owner of a stock and sees its value begin to rise and fall, he begins to get nervous and make mistakes, although in fact this process does not mean anything. It's normal for a stock to fall in value and doesn't mean you should get rid of it. Of course, the company may eventually go bankrupt, but Buffett again advises diversification. It is possible to make a very large income even if three out of four companies in which you own shares are not in very good shape. It is only important to recognize where there is high volatility and where there are signs of a company's collapse.

Invest for the long term

This is another habit that distinguishes a financially literate person from an illiterate one. A financially illiterate person does not know how to wait. When he sees that he can make a 25% profit a year after the purchase, he immediately sells all his shares. A financially savvy person will wait much longer and ultimately make a huge profit. There is no point in investing in securities if your ultimate dream is 25% profit. This can also be achieved in less risky financial transactions.

This rule applies not only to the securities market, but to business and money in general.

There is not much difference between a large and a small investor

This refers to both psychological behavior and the threshold for entry into this area. In addition, small investors can unite. Which, however, leads to some understandable shortcomings.

Avoid companies that make expensive purchases

When a company lists its shares on the stock exchange, everyone starts buying them, and that company makes huge profits. Then human psychology begins to work again . Heads of companies or CEOs become blind and do not understand the difference between the already mentioned price and value. They see that people are buying their shares for a lot of money, and they think that this is what speaks of their success, although who, if not the head of the companies, should know how things really are?

Therefore, such companies begin to soar in the skies, allow themselves big expenses, inflate their staff and behave as befits someone who has had huge amounts of money from others fall on their head, i.e. unreasonable. You always need to watch how the company will behave after placing its shares on the stock exchange. You need to recognize a competent leader and then buy shares of his company.

These seven rules of Warren Buffett will help every person succeed not only when investing their money in stocks, but also in any business, because... these two areas are inextricably linked. Now let's move on to generating passive income. We will first of all touch upon investments.

It is worth saying right away that in many cases you will have to work and think a lot before you start receiving passive income. To think about this, you need financial literacy. This is why you need to go through the entire course, because simply listing ways to make money will not work. You need to develop a financial mindset before you try to invest your money.

The good news is that before you save up enough money to invest, your thinking can and should undergo quite a few changes in the meantime. Determine in advance the amount of passive income you need to quit your five-day job and start doing what you've always dreamed of. And, best of all, you can engage in self-development , which many people do not do because they work from morning to night.

We invite you to solve a short case to understand how ready you are to invest.

Sources of passive and conditionally passive income

Bank deposit
This is the simplest and least profitable investment. On the other hand, with compound interest, things get a lot more interesting.

Compound interest is when you earn interest on the interest you make on your deposits. Those. if you put $100,000 in the bank at 10% interest, after a year you have $110,000. Let's assume that you did not withdraw your interest - then after another year the interest is calculated from 110 thousand and will be 121 thousand dollars. In two years your income will be equal to 21 thousand dollars. If you keep your deposit for 5 years, the amount will be 161 thousand dollars. The longer the period, the greater the amount will be.

Sometimes the amount of interest is calculated every month, which means that there will be even more money. In this case, the amount after five years will be 165, not 161 thousand dollars. Google "Online Compound Interest Calculator" and in a few seconds calculate your potential profit at a specific rate. In some cases, you can put additional money on your deposit, and it will also work for you. Online calculators can calculate this too.

The advantages of compound interest are also an extension of its disadvantages. Compound interest is only good for long-term investments. And long-term investments are very risky. However, economists say that after global crises, the world economy recovers and you can put money in the bank for a long time without fear of consequences.

You can consider bank deposits from a diversification perspective. If you have the opportunity, put the money in the bank, but not first, but after you have created several other sources of passive income.

Starting your own company

This is a form of conditional passive income. At first, you will have to work and analyze a lot. As in any business, serious risks are possible, and one of the main requirements is the ability to motivate and manage people. In this lesson, we talked about the cash flow quadrant, where we saw a clear difference between a small and a large businessman - the first one works only for himself, is busy almost the whole day and cannot even afford vacations. Therefore, in our case, it is important to create a company that will help you, if you wish, spend all your time there or engage in travel and self-development.

This approach is practiced by Richard Branson . This is a British entrepreneur and owner of 400 companies of various profiles. Surprisingly, this person finds a lot of free time, travels around the world, enjoys life and is a truly happy person. This is an ideal businessman in terms of financial literacy: he has reached incredible heights, receives phenomenal profits and takes everything from life. The corporation complements him, not he the corporation. Surely you have seen other businessmen who are constantly working and always look emotionally burnt out. This is not about Richard Branson.

However, a company can also be an Internet site. It is good because, with proper development, it can generate stable passive income and usually does not require serious intervention. If your site is popular enough, you can hire someone you trust to manage the site and then only make occasional adjustments. Some businessmen are the owners of dozens of websites, some of which only support the popularity and influence of others.

Resale of real estate

When is the best time to buy real estate? Right now. Practice shows that real estate prices always rise. Just remember Warren Buffett's rule and don't confuse price and value.

Someone is engaged in buying and selling real estate, starting with the acquisition of inexpensive apartments or land. This is why you will most likely need other sources of income.

And to understand how you can buy and sell real estate with virtually no capital, read Robert Allen's book, Multiple Streams of Income. Allen points out an obvious point that often goes unnoticed: You'll have to spend many months trying to find that one home that's worth less than it should be. It's a lot of work, but the rewards can be incredible. There will always be accommodating and compliant real estate sellers everywhere. This could be a person who is moving abroad and urgently needs to sell his own house. Or maybe this is a person who has been trying to sell real estate for too long and is ready for certain conditions.

You will need to study the real estate market very seriously and learn to distinguish a good deal from a bad deal. Make a list of the advantages that the house should have, and estimate what amount in this case will suit you. At first, it may seem that it is impossible to find such real estate, but you must understand that patience will pay off several times over, you just need to not give up. There will always be people who are ready to bargain and agree to your terms. Creating a trusting relationship will be the first step towards this.

Therefore, if you managed to purchase a house, do not rush to reduce your stated price. You have time, the more it works for you. In the meantime, you are waiting for a buyer, you can use the following advice.

Renting out real estate

This form of passive income is the simplest (if you have it, of course). In this case, you must not only rent out the property, but also monitor the market to see if it can be sold at a profit.

People who resell real estate often rent it out. It already brings in passive income, and they are quietly looking for a buyer. Therefore, the most competent behavior would be to sell the property for an amount that will be more profitable than renting it out for a year or two.

It is difficult to say whether expensive repairs are necessary before selling, but cosmetic repairs are simply necessary. For a small price, you can turn a bad apartment into a normal one, which will allow you to rent it out for a higher price.

This type of passive income is very attractive and also has very few risks.

Copyright

Here are four types of activities that are subject to copyright:

1. Writing a book, script, or manual; development of methodology, model, and computer program. This type is good because all income goes only to you. You can now even sell your book on Amazon. If you publish it, you will also receive royalties for reprints.
2. Writing music, song lyrics, symphony, sound bank. When using Youtube you can become very famous if you are talented. Just 20 years ago this was simply impossible.

3. Invention of useful things, devices, structures. You don't need to be a scientist, physicist, or genius. Sometimes even a simple but very necessary thing for humanity brings its creator millions.
4. Patenting of other property rights. Photos, videos, video tutorials, drawings.

We live in a very interesting world in which people don't like copyrights. Perhaps this is correct. These features of the twenty-first century are used by many financially and psychologically literate people. Some people simply give their first works to humanity and create a name for themselves. And someone protects any of their work in such a way that people turn away from the creator and his product. The first type of people seems to be winning. In the age of the Internet and information, name and fame mean an incredible amount, so use copyright wisely. Otherwise, you will remain the only person on the planet who uses your invention.

Shares and securities

Securities are commodity or monetary documents that give their owner property rights and the right to receive certain amounts of money and income ("Modern Economic Dictionary", B. Raizberg, L. Lozovsky, E. Starodubtseva). Securities include shares, bonds (bonds), bills of exchange, and cash checks.

We will not advise you on how you can make money by playing on the stock exchange. And almost no one else can guarantee you anything. Robert Allen, in his book Multiple Streams of Income, concludes that this is a very complex type of investment in which there is almost no one hundred percent winning strategy. Market players who showed excellent results in the previous period will very likely not show any serious results in this one. Of course, there are strategies with minimal risks, but the profits will be quite small. Therefore, when starting to play on the stock exchange, be prepared for all possible scenarios.

We have already learned one rule of playing on the stock exchange from Warren Buffett - stocks are worth buying for a long period. This is approximately 10-20 years. The second rule concerns the speculative value of a stock, in which case profits can be made very quickly simply because the price of one share of a particular company can be artificially inflated. The art of playing on the stock exchange depends on understanding where you need to be guided by the first and whereby the second rule.

When playing on the stock exchange, there are many tools that we suggest you study on your own. But remember: a huge number of people have failed on the stock market. Some even believe that the stock exchange is no different from betting at the racetrack or playing dice. We suggest you engage in this type of investment last when you become a fairly wealthy person. Or proceed at your peril and risk.

Buying a franchise

Franchising is the purchase of a developed business model and obtaining rights to a certain type of business. Those. you can buy the rights to trademarks and brands of a particular company and make money from it. There are two disadvantages to buying a franchise: the high price and possible difficulties when transferring from another country. But there is also a significant advantage: a ready-made business model. Staff training takes place according to a pre-developed methodology, and besides, you, do not need advertising if you bought the rights from a well-known company.

FINANCIAL OUTLOOK

Before buying a franchise, you need to spend a lot of time studying and analyzing the activities of this company (we will touch on this topic in the fifth lesson), as well as identifying all the pitfalls in connection with the transfer of a franchise from one country to another. There can be a lot of legal subtleties.

You can pay attention to whether someone else has bought this franchise in your country. If you bought it, then determine how successful this purchase was.

The license usually takes into account four points:

- Franchise cost.
- Mandatory initial capital. It can be 10-20 times higher than the cost of the franchise.
- Royalties (monthly payments).
- Duration of the franchise agreement.

As you can see, the conditions are indeed very strict. For example, the cost of a McDonald's franchise is only 45-50 thousand dollars, but a large number of little things are included in the rights transfer agreement, which ultimately eats up an amount several times greater than the cost of the franchise itself.

But if you succeed, within 5-10 years you will begin to receive passive income and only occasionally direct your company in the right direction.

Blog and YouTube channel

Another type of conditional passive income. It will take you some time to start generating income from every blog post or YouTube video. These two ways of earning money can hardly be called basic and sufficient, but they can be additional.

In this case, you need to be different from everything that other people do, and at the same time absorb the best strategies. Earnings may vary, but some people earn around $200-$300 per month and still invest a small amount of time into promoting their blog or channel.

7

The Power of Positive Thinking

Surely many of you have already heard more than once about the benefits of positive thinking. But what does this mean? And how to completely get rid of negative thoughts? Few people understand this. In this article, we'll look at the benefits of positive thoughts and exercises to practice positive thinking.

Positive thinking benefits not only a person's psyche and intellect but also his health. What are the real benefits of positive thinking:

- Stress resistance increases;
- The risk of depression is reduced;
- You will be able to cope with various negative conditions faster;
- Life expectancy increases;
- You will become more confident in yourself, willpower and motivation will increase;
- You will be able to better concentrate on tasks and achieve goals.

But there is an important condition! It is necessary to let all positive thoughts pass through yourself, and not just seem cheerful and hide behind the sign of success. After all, when negativity is boiling inside you and you try to suppress it with a frozen smile, this can only lead to disastrous consequences, for example, psychosomatic illnesses. Therefore, it is important to work through your internal state, your thoughts, and your emotions. When harmony, calm, and balance appear inside, then externally you will begin to radiate happiness and positivity.

Practice positive thinking

Praise yourself for everything, even the smallest achievements or failures

It's easy to thank yourself for big victories, but noticing small achievements and finding the good in failures is not an easy task. It is important to learn how to correctly analyze any situation, thereby turning it into experience and wisdom. Force yourself to look for 5 moments every day for which you could praise yourself. It is better if you write them out and keep a diary in this way.

Describe your ideal day

This is an effective exercise to understand what you want and are constantly avoiding. Imagine your ideal day, think through the important points, and try to implement it shortly. Afterward, analyze this day, if something did not work out, then re-write all the moments and bring them to life. Then think about the emotions and feelings you experienced. Train yourself to live your ideal day as often as possible, and then you will see qualitative changes in yourself afterward.

Manage your thoughts anons

Negative emotions and thoughts suck all the vital energy out of us.

But these same thoughts are born in our heads, so we can learn to control them. A person can manage and control his thoughts at any moment in life, but this requires practice. By the way, this is not as difficult as it might seem. Step-by-step instructions for developing emotional intelligence are in the free course " Emotional Intelligence ".

Write down 5 positive things

This is a fairly well-known technique and works. You need to find 5 positive aspects in any event, preferably in the worst one. And you will be surprised that even in the most hopeless situations you can find positive, heartfelt moments for yourself. You will also see the situation from the other side, and find non-standard solutions and opportunities.

Make peace with the past

Often negative thoughts stem from unpleasant events from a past life. A person constantly returns mentally to this moment, gets upset, and spoils his mood, depriving himself of strength and energy. Try to let go of the past, forgive old grievances, start living in the present, change yourself, and don't become a hostage to past failures.

8

Mastering Money Habits

Together with experts, we studied 10 financial habits that you need to master by the age of 20 in order to properly build your financial future.

1. Know your strengths and weaknesses

Knowing your pros and cons when it comes to money is key to achieving financial wellness. Who are you - a spender or a hoarder? Can you save money? Can you refuse unplanned expenses or, on the contrary, are your desires your main priority? Are you familiar with the basic financial instruments? Do you know how to use credit cards? How well do you understand market economics? The answers to these and some other questions form your financial profile.

Renat Abilkadilov, business coach at the Business Perspective center: "Financial profile is your attitude towards money. And it is not always possible to determine this relationship the first time; moreover, it is not always unambiguous and unchangeable. Find out your attitude towards finance - this will help you correctly formulate your desires, set goals and build motivation to achieve them."

2. Give up bad habits

Impulsive, momentary purchases are not conducive to wealth accumulation. Give up this bad habit, otherwise by the age of thirty, this behavior - succumbing to the weaknesses of shopping - will provide you with lasting financial problems.

Elena Poniznikova, psychologist: "The problem is not that you are shopping. The problem is that you believe that these purchases will make you happy. Shopping as an ersatz happiness is just a temporary satiation, like satisfying hunger with sweet soda: after a few sips it seems that hunger has subsided, but after a few minutes it returns with a vengeance."

3. Be able to control expenses

How to wisely cut costs

Control over spending is the key to financial stability. This is one of the key financial habits, the development of which will be the key to future stability. Within ten years - you reach the age of thirty - the ability to control expenses should become an integral part of your life.

Petr Klimenko, author of business training on financial planning: "Spending less than you earn is the main way to become the master of your life. Control your habits, know how to plan your income and expenses - and you will get ahead."

4. Remember about debts

Debt management is a financial tool like any other. And a loan can become both a salvation in a difficult situation, and the stone that will drag you to the bottom.

Anton Gorlikov, a financial consultant at the Vicks and Sons consulting agency: "There is a simple rule in competent debt management: do not invest borrowed money in rapidly depreciating assets. It's easy to determine: are you taking out a loan to buy something - a phone, a watch, branded shoes? It means you can't afford it, don't buy it."

Max Reznik, entrepreneur, and coach: "Bad debts are debts for clothes, food, entertainment, telephone, TV or car. Good debts - loans for housing, business, investments, education. Are you borrowing money for other purposes? You don't know how to handle money."

5. Know how to save

It is important to develop the habit of saving, to look for benefits where in a normal situation you would not see them.

Greg Loughlin, professor of economics, University of Southern California: "Saving is a habit that can be called the basis of personal financial education. The ability to save develops an internal sense of order and helps in achieving goals."

6. Save for the future

How to become a millionaire: 3 principles of savings

A financial "airbag" or money "for a rainy day" is protecting your future. At twenty years old, it's time to give up the habit of relying on your parents and hoping for their immediate help in difficult situations that arise. Having a certain amount that can "save" during a personal financial crisis is a sign of maturity and independence.

Anton Gorlikov, a financial consultant at the consulting agency "Vicks and Sons": "Your financial future is being laid right now, at 20-25. Your future capital will depend on how you master financial instruments."

7. Strive for financial independence

Of course, it is difficult to completely abandon the financial support of your parents at the age of twenty. However, at this age, it is already necessary to provide for daily expenses on your own. Even with full-time study at a university, students are provided with many opportunities to earn money.

Maxim Reznik, entrepreneur, and coach: "Bad debts and the habit of relying on parents are a reason for panic. Parents are not an ATM!"

8. Be able to set goals

Vladimir Gerasichev: "Who said that we need to fight laziness"

Much has already been said about the fact that the correct formulation of the problem is already half the success. But still, financial advisors never tire of repeating: clarity in setting goals helps in achieving them.

Renat Abilkadilov: "The main component of financial stability is the ability to quickly, clearly and formulate your desires. But do not forget that goals, first of all, must be practical. We set a specific task and look for ways to solve it - that's what goal setting is."

9. Get rid of laziness

Procrastination or postponing for later is the same laziness. The key to financial success is the ability to put "I have to" above my own "I don't want to." You can't make money without leaving your parents' couch.

Elena Poniznikova: "Twenty years is the time to get rid of the internal protest that has developed due to parental pressure: "You have to go to school," "You have to learn your homework," "You have to wash the dishes." All these personal compulsions only clog the psyche, preparing the ground for problems in the future. The task of young people is to throw out all this mental garbage."

10. Know how to share

Charity is not a thoughtless waste of money, but an opportunity to receive it. One of the opportunities that charity gives is an attempt to learn how to manage cash flow.

Olga Kuznetsova, psychologist: "In modern society, money is considered an analog of happiness. How often do we hear: "If only I had a lot of money, I would be happy." That is, a simple chain arises: have money - spend it - enjoy the purchase. An effective recipe to get rid of this addiction is to try to break one of the links in the chain. For example, replacing pointless purchases by donating money to charity."

FINANCIAL OUTLOOK

The main thing you need to learn by age twenty is to realize that time is the most valuable asset you have. Time is the main advantage of 20-year-olds. At this age, you can afford to make mistakes, including money ones. However, we should not forget that smart financial habits, which will become the basis for well-being, are laid precisely at this age.

9

Fixed Mindset

The main idea of Carol Dweck's very popular book "The New Psychology of Success. Think and Win" comes down to the fact that there are two types of thinking: the first makes a person degrade and blame everyone around him for his failures, while the second leads to personal growth and responsibility for his life. Today we will talk in detail about the first of them because you need to know the enemy by sight.

People with a fixed mindset believe that their abilities are "set in stone," meaning they cannot change throughout their lives. They don't work on their development. People with a growth mindset, on the other hand, believe that they can learn anything and master almost any skill. They believe that their basic abilities are just a starting point.

Despite its name, a fixed mindset can be changed. This is just a set of habitual attitudes that we unconsciously apply when faced with problems, failures, and criticism addressed to us.

Below we list the disadvantages of a fixed mindset:

- A person tries to hide his shortcomings so that he is not judged and called a failure.
- He tries to adhere to the rules, knowledge, and experience that he has because this is how (in his opinion) he can maintain self-confidence.
- He believes that mistakes speak volumes about his personality.
- Thinks that if he fails, then all his efforts and time are wasted.

In short, a fixed mindset does not allow a person to realize his potential, limits him, and narrows his worldview.

If you notice signs of it in yourself, it's time to change your thinking, and therefore your life, for the better.

A Step-by-Step Process for Changing a Fixed Mindset

The key to changing your thinking lies primarily in awareness.

To change fixed thinking, you need to learn to identify the situations that cause it. Carol Dweck herself suggests four steps for this.

Step One: Learn to Hear the "Voice" of the Fixed Mindset
When a new challenge approaches, this voice may say, "Are you sure you can do this?" Or, "What if you fail?"
After the first serious failure, you may hear: "Oh, if only you had talent…". Or: "I told you it was too risky."

Some business coaches talk about him as an internal saboteur. It is the voice that undermines everything we do; the inner critic who judges us and our work.

This inner saboteur is the fixed mindset. Once you can recognize his voice, move on to step two.

Step Two: Recognize You Have a Choice
You can interpret this voice in two different ways:

Problems, failures, and criticism can be a sign that you have "fixed" your talent and abilities.
Or it could be a sign that you need to challenge yourself, step up your efforts, change your strategy, and keep growing.
Obviously, in the first case, we are talking about a fixed mindset, in the second - about a growth mindset.

Remember, you always have a choice when faced with a failure, problem, or criticism.

Step Three: Respond with a Growth Mindset Voice
When you encounter a problem, the voice of the fixed mindset says, "Are you sure you can do this? Do you have enough abilities and talent?

The growth mindset responds, "I'm not sure I can handle this right now, but I think I can learn over time with the necessary effort."

The fixed mindset insists, "But what if you fail? You will become a loser!"

And the growth mindset answers: "All successful people have failed, and more than one. However, this did not make them failures."

If you do fail, the fixed mindset will again say, "I told you so. You have no ability."

But you can counter this thought with the voice of growth thinking: "This is all nonsense. Science was difficult for Thomas Edison, and Michael Jordan did not immediately become a brilliant basketball player. But what they had in abundance was a passion for their hobby and a lot of effort."

If you face criticism, the limiting voice says, "It's not my fault. It's all other people and circumstances that influenced it."

This can be answered as follows: "If I don't take responsibility, I won't be able to fix it. I will listen carefully to criticism and learn from my mistakes."

It is very convenient to write such dialogues in your diary. This will allow you to come up with not just one refutation, but dozens.

Step Four: Develop New Thinking
When you hear the voice of a fixed mindset and respond to it with a growth mindset, instead of stopping your progress, you begin to take the necessary proactive actions.
Actions can be understood as:

- Accepting new challenges;
- Learning from failures and mistakes;
- Showing persistence

Adjusting your actions based on feedback.

Step Five: Ask the Right Questions
Despite the serial number, this is the most important tip. Thinking can be changed for the better with the right questions, just as it can be limited.

Here is a list of questions to help you develop a growth mindset:

1. What steps can I take to be successful?
2. What can I learn from this situation?
3. Am I aware of my end goal when I do something?
4. What additional information will help me?
5. Where can I get constructive feedback?
6. What do I need to do, how can I change my daily routine to follow the plan?
7. How exactly will I implement the plan?
8. What new did I learn today? About myself, about life, about people.
9. What mistakes did I make today? What conclusions did you draw?
10. Is my current strategy working? If not, how can I change it?
11. What do I need to work hard on today?
12. What habits should I develop and what skills should I master to reach my goal faster?

Questions determine your focus and greatly influence your perception of reality. The more often you ask them, the wider, brighter, and richer your life will become.

10

Money Management

Financial literacy is not something fantastic, it is simply knowledge of some principles. They are not a secret and you can find some excellent advice in many books on the subject. However, it is impossible to do without an integrated approach, because half-measures cannot give the desired result.

We have collected most of these tips in this article and will consider each of them separately. But first, let's talk about why many people fail to be financially literate. Or rather, about the excuses that people come up with for themselves.

Excuses for Financial illiteracy

Psychological excuses

It's all about how we look at wealth accumulation. For example, you may have many limiting beliefs about money that have been ingrained in your psyche over many years as a result of your upbringing or traumatic events.

It should be said right away that beliefs affect the way you look at money - both for the better and for the worse. Here's what they can be:

- Money is the root of all evil.
- I will not like the life of a rich man, he has too many problems, and I am free.
- You have to work hard into old age to become rich.
- To make money, you need money.
- To become rich, you need to cheat, lie and steal.
- I'm not smart enough to be rich.

These beliefs are deeply rooted in the psyche and often get in the way of making good financial decisions.

Physical Excuses

These are addictions for which we ourselves are to blame. For example, watching TV, surfing the Internet without purpose or meaning, playing video games, impulse purchases. They distract from thoughts about becoming a wealthy person, that is, they become a kind of defense mechanisms.

Social excuses

These excuses usually come in the form of the phrase: "I don't have the right connections to become rich." To some extent, this may be true, because the people with whom you communicate determine your thinking.

But this is still an excuse. Especially in the information world, where with due persistence you can meet, if not the greatest businessmen, then at least quite ambitious ones.

You need to stop making excuses for yourself. Firmly decide that you are ready to change your thinking - this is the best thing you can do. And it may take years, but it will pay off in full.

How to learn to manage money

Start budgeting

A budget is not only an accounting of income and expenses, but also a plan for saving money and investing.

Many financial experts believe that the budget should be maintained according to the 60/30/10 principle:

- 60% of the income should go to your needs;
- 30% of your income should go towards your desires;
- 10% of your income needs to be put aside.

However, if you want to become financially independent, you need to put yourself in more difficult conditions. For example, the budget can look like 50/10/40 or even 50/5/45. It all depends on your living conditions, income and expenses.

Of course, you need to not only keep records, but also manage your finances. The following information is about exactly this.

Minimize your monthly expenses

This should become a habit. Once a week, think about what expenses you can cut. At the same time, it is important to be in a good mood and not think that you are making sacrifices. Turn the process into a game.

Here are three key questions to help you stick to this rule:

- Do I really need this?
- Can I do without this?
- What are my options?

Save money

The more money you have saved, the stronger your financial situation. To properly tune your thinking , ask yourself the following questions:

- Why do I want to start saving?
- Why is this important to me?
- What are the long-term consequences of such a habit?
- We'll talk more about this a little later.

Spend only your money

No matter how much advertising assures you of the profitability of the next loan offer, even if there is a need to take advantage of it, approach it carefully.

It doesn't take much intelligence to borrow and manage other people's money. This habit leads to incorrect thinking, and even to debt. We will also talk about this topic later.

Create a Financial Cushion

A financial cushion should be understood as the amount of money on which you could live for 6 months if you lose your job or lose all sources of income. This time is needed not only to find a new job, but also to find yourself, develop skills, study, and read.

Some people create a financial cushion just in order to temporarily retire and engage in self-development or, for example, write a book. This is also a great solution, just remember that it will not be too easy to return.

Calculating the financial cushion is quite easy, although some people use long formulas. Find out how much money you need to live for a month - just calculate your expenses for the last six months and take the average. This way you will get an approximate final result.

Of course, the financial cushion does not take into account inflation, price increases and unforeseen circumstances, so it is more correct to add a reserve fund to it. Here you are free to decide whether you need to create it and, if so, how much money should be contributed to it.

Set financial goals

Psychologically, it is very difficult to save money or save money if you don't have any goals. The question constantly arises in my head: "Why am I suffering so much?" When you don't find the answer, you give up.

So set yourself financial goals. Here are examples:

Become financially independent

This means receiving enough passive income to become independent from work. You can quit and live peacefully on the money that regularly goes into your pocket.

How much money do you need per month to feel good? Write down this amount. After that, start thinking about what you need to do to get that passive income.

Get financial protection

It's a simple goal: how much money do you need to cover all your monthly needs and save a certain amount? For example, you earn a thousand dollars, of which you save two hundred dollars every month. You spend the rest. If this is enough, it means that you are financially protected and are able to feed yourself at this stage of life.

Get financial security

This is a certain amount of money that will allow you not to depend on other people. It is needed if you want, say, to go to India for a year to get acquainted with the culture of this country and indulge in spiritual practices. How much money do you need to quit and not ask anyone for money?

We previously wrote about the financial cushion and reserve fund. These are also goals that you can and should set for yourself.

How to learn to save money

Are you saving money? If so, do you think you can increase this percentage? Do you save where others impulsively spend and then regret it?

These are all questions that you need to give yourself an honest answer to right now. The habit of saving money is very difficult to develop. And that is why there are so few rich people in the world. This requires a different kind of thinking that will lead to completely different decisions throughout the day.

However, if you want to achieve financial freedom, the first thing you must do is start saving some of your income. You will think about what to do with them later.

To start saving money, you need to save. This does not mean that your life will immediately turn into hell: for this you do not need to go on a hunger strike and go to live in the forest.

Create your saving plan

First of all, set achievable goals and commit to saving a certain amount of money (or transferring it to a bank you trust).

It is believed that every person, if he works, can save 10% of his income. You don't need to dramatically increase this number right away, but try going to 15-20%.

Think Economically

Whenever we hear that a person is thrifty, we immediately begin to consider him a miser. Sometimes this is true, so try to clearly define: what does frugality mean to you?

For example, frugal people tend to:

- Cook at home instead of ordering food or dining out.
- Use free apps instead of paid ones.
- Exercise outside instead of buying expensive gym memberships. Some people even think in the spirit of: "If I buy a membership, I will definitely go to the gym so that it won't be so offensive."
- Buy good and not expensive clothes (and there are such things).
- Borrow books from the library rather than buy them.

Perhaps you think it's important to buy books because you love self-development and just reading. In this case, do not use the last advice, it is not an axiom.

Overall, these are just a few examples. We believe that you can create a personal list by analyzing your behavior over the past month. Think about how much money you have wasted before, and then start saving it. A decent amount will accrue in a year (yes, we have already said that accumulation is a long process).

Consider working remotely

Instead of wasting time and money commuting to the office, try convincing your employer that you can do all your work at home (at least 1-2 days a week). This way you will save, including a lot of time. However, keep in mind that working at home is not easy - you will have to learn to motivate yourself.

Play sports to prevent illness

We rarely think about it, but we should. The US is experiencing a boom in interest in sports, since medicine there is so expensive that it can make almost anyone bankrupt if they start getting sick often (insurance does not cover all cases).

Therefore, be smarter too. The body wears out one way or another. To slow down this unpleasant process, you need to exercise and take care of your health: take care of your body and your teeth, stop drinking and smoking, and switch to healthy foods. After all, what's the point of earning a lot of money now if you end up spending it all on treatment?

How to get rid of debts

Our tips are aimed at managing the money you have. But what to do if you are deeply in debt? What strategy is needed?

You can use the following 7-step program. However, this does not mean that it will be easy. Quite the contrary. Any difficult situation is different in that you first need to change your thinking, and not act according to the usual algorithms.

Step One: Admit There Is a Problem

If you live in debt most of your life, it can become a habit and create a parasitic mindset. You need to get rid of it as quickly as possible.

First, openly admit that there is a problem.
Take full responsibility. Whatever happened in the past, you are somehow to blame for it. Forgive yourself for this. You got a second chance and won't make those mistakes again.

Acknowledging the problem helps to create new thinking and get rid of whining and blaming.

Step two: take inventory
What we mean here is this: list all your debts. With knowledge comes power. When you understand who you owe and how much, you can pull yourself together and make more informed financial decisions.

List your debts, starting with the smallest and ending with the largest. Then clearly decide how much money you will allocate to repayment each week or each month.

The idea is to pay off your smallest debts first. This way you will reduce the number of creditors. This will relieve stress and allow you to focus on just a few people.

Step Three: Eliminate Everything Non-essential
Start living frugally. Sit down, think a little, and make a plan for what areas of your life you can cut back on.

This is one of the most unpleasant stages, but it is necessary. Stop feeling sorry for yourself and give up unnecessary pleasures. Leave the essentials. Don't buy anything you can't survive without.

Step Four: Create a Realistic Spending Plan
This is a budget in which you set monthly limits on categories of items and services. You must be strict with yourself. Once you indulge yourself, the process will spin out of control. You know how this happens.

Step five: sell everything you don't need
Let's now get out of debt by adding some cash to our pocket. Selling necessary things is the last thing, but you can get rid of unnecessary things without losing self-esteem.

Make a list of such things. You will be surprised, but you can earn a decent amount if you manage to sell it all.

Thus, your apartment will become more spacious, which will have a positive effect on the quality of thinking.

Step Six: Think about how to increase your income
At this stage you need to turn on your thinking to the fullest. There are probably some ways to earn something quickly without taking a second job.

Sit down and write down a list of a hundred ways to make money. It seems impossible, but if you just think a little, it turns out that there are a lot of opportunities around.

As a last resort, talk to your boss. Perhaps he can provide additional work or help you find something else.

Step Seven: Find Support
It is not easy to cope with such a period of life alone. Therefore, ask your loved ones for support. Explain to them that you need them and that you want to get out of the debt hole. Some of them may even help you find a part-time job.

11

Wealth-Building Strategies

To succeed at anything, you need to develop a plan. This works in sports, career, and personal development, and it is also incredibly relevant in business. If you don't have a plan or strategy, then you take pointless actions in hopes of achieving your goals. This is reminiscent of playing roulette. Of course, this approach in business is sometimes even useful, especially for people with excellent intuition, but to learn it, you still have to create a business strategy, implement it, and gain a lot of experience. This chapter provides you with a smart, systematic approach to developing it.

Approaches to Strategy

Depending on the scope of your ambitions and circumstances, you can develop strategies to:

- Increase profitability
- Gain a larger market share
- Increase customer satisfaction
- Complete the project within budget

To define your strategy, you must identify the external and internal factors that will influence it. With this approach, you will be able to recognize opportunities and use them for your success.

Creating a strategy is a three-step process:

- Analysis of the situation and environment
- Defining strategic options
- Evaluation and selection of the best option

Let's look at each step separately, as well as several useful techniques that will help you develop a strategy.

Analyze the situation and surroundings

Do the following:

Analyze your company's activities Explore resources, opportunities, strengths, and weaknesses. SWOT analysis is a great technique for just this.

Analyze your environment Are there any opportunities in the market? What will happen in the future in your industry and how will it affect your business? PEST analysis is a great starting point for environmental analysis. You must adapt to your environment, not go against it.

Analyze customers and stakeholders Strategy determines exactly how you are going to win the market game. One of the best ways to do this is to satisfy your customers. What do they want? Also think about meeting the expectations of your shareholders, investors, and partner companies.

Analyze your competitors Develop competitive intelligence. This will help you study the strengths and weaknesses of other companies and develop a strategy accordingly. Answer the questions: How easy is it to enter your market? What alternatives do your clients have?

Identify Strategic Options

It's time to find ideas that will help you gain a competitive advantage and achieve your goals.

Brainstorm and come up with several options You can use reverse brainstorming techniques to explore projects that you can launch and gain a competitive advantage. Define your boundaries, and then look for options within them.

Explore opportunities and threats SWOT analysis will also help in this case. Make a complete list of them, and then maximize the benefits and minimize the threats. At best, turn the latter into the former.

Solve problems You will solve problems every day, but some situations can be prevented. First, you need to find and formulate a problem. The " Five Whys " technique will help you with this - it was created to find the root of the problem using questions.

Evaluate and select the best strategic options

Now you have several strategies, but you need to work them out in detail so that you can then evaluate, compare, and choose.

Development of options Some strategies seem attractive until they begin to be developed. And vice versa. So use the mind map method to create a rough outline of each strategy. Don't try to evaluate or compare them at this stage, just go to the end.

Evaluate and choose the best strategies Of course, ideally, a strategy should require fewer resources and produce more results. However, this rarely happens; more often than not, you have to compare several different strategies without any obvious advantage of one over the other. Think about your company's goals and mission: are there strategies that conflict with them? However, you can change your goals and missions or modify them.

Implementation of strategy
To correctly implement the strategy, answer the following questions:

- What are your strengths and weaknesses?
- Are you able to achieve the goal and implement the strategy?
- Do you see the big picture of trends in your industry?
- How will you observe and analyze external factors?
- Who are the people on whom the implementation of the strategy depends?
- What choice do you have?

There is no such thing as "right" or "wrong" when it comes to strategy.

Even a strategy that seems bad on paper can be profitable. If you clearly understand your strategy, you will be able to implement it, despite obstacles and threats from all sides.

12

Bad Financial Habits

Cultivating good habits is just as important as eliminating bad ones. When it comes to finances, the rates rise exponentially. Small expenses that could have been avoided ultimately lead to a person getting into debt and not having control over his life. Let's try to become financially literate people and start by getting rid of habits that threaten to make our lives worse.

Habits tend to form automatically, without our participation. And wherever there is unconsciousness, there will be people who will take advantage of it. We present to your attention seven bad habits that you urgently need to get rid of.

Impulse purchase

A person who does not have a financial goal will make such purchases again and again. During impulse purchases, we lose touch with our budget, which leads not only to its depletion but also to unnecessary loans. Never make such purchases. If you see something that you suddenly want to buy, take a break for a few days. Marketers also take this into account, so they force you to hurry because otherwise, the price of this thing will increase - so you need to buy it here and now. Don't fall for such tricks. The world is filled with goods and if you still need it, you can buy it at any time. Do not buy an item before you can earn money for it (for example, on credit). It is better to refrain from this and carefully consider whether this money can be spent on something more useful.

Keep up with your friend

Competition is good in matters of business, self-development, and personal growth. We all want to become better than others and this is a completely normal process. When it comes to shopping, a person may spend more than necessary simply to impress others. The big problem is that no one admits why they bought an unnecessary thing. The person will make excuses and sincerely believe that he needs her and that he does not want to make an impression. Be honest with yourself.

When someone you know buys an expensive item, it can trigger a psychological trigger to do the same, to compete with him. Look at anything for the opportunities it opens up for you, and not for its appearance. Find out if there is another similar thing, but much cheaper.

Remember that success is difficult to evaluate from the outside. The person who buys expensive things may be much poorer than you. Completely different things are said about the true state of affairs, and over a long distance.

Shopping for joy

Shopping is generally considered a psychological illness, although some people can be convinced that it is a lifestyle. There is nothing more financially wrong than enjoying the act of shopping. Better read a book or do yoga. Shopping temporarily relieves the problems that it causes.

Other things will pump endorphins into your brain without costing you a penny. When you go shopping to lift your spirits, you create a clear and simple association command for your brain (anchoring method in NLP) - shopping is a pleasure. This leads to the fact that nothing else excites you more than shopping. Then this connection becomes extremely difficult to break.

Before buying, ask yourself whether you need this item or if you just want to temporarily improve your mood. 100 dollars for a good mood - isn't that a lot to pay? Moreover, you could spend a week of your life earning such a sum. However, if you decide for yourself that you need this item, buy it and have fun. But at the same time, the value of this thing must correspond to its price.

Waiting for a miracle

Many people associate buying an item with a miracle, some great joy. Such dependence on things makes life difficult for any person and will never make him truly happy. Happiness always sits within and depends little on external factors.

Often, buying a new thing brings a lot of problems, in addition to additional expenses for its maintenance. Disappointment sets in, after which the person thinks about how to correct the situation - and yet another purchase comes to the rescue. This chain will never be broken if you continue to expect miracles from your purchases.

Desire for a rich lifestyle

As we get older, we expect a better financial status in life than we had when we were younger. Better job, more income, great opportunities. However, many people mistakenly believe that they only need money to spend it instantly. The problem doesn't arise when you spend a lot and still earn the same amount. It occurs when at some point in your life you are fired from your job or your income drops. At this point, you begin to regret not investing your money in your future when you had it. Confidence that you can earn more and more every year is an irrational approach to life, although correct from a motivational point of view. Earn more, but don't let yourself spend all your money. A rich man does not have a car, but one who can quit his job and live off the interest on his investments.

Keep your debts out of your sight

Of course, if you have debt, it shouldn't eat you up inside. You can move on with your life, but remember that you need to get rid of him as quickly as possible. Loans and debts have one simple feature - the sooner you pay them off, the better. Get rid of debt and start planning your budget.

The very presence of debt makes a person emotionally unstable and easily susceptible to stress. It affects a person most destructively. Be aware of your debts and get rid of them.

Take interest-free loans

This is the most tricky type of loan. Everything about it seems great, but its very presence contradicts one of the most important laws of financial literacy - don't buy something you haven't earned for. Of course, even here there are exceptions when buying this thing will allow you to make money on it, but still, usually, a person buys a completely unnecessary thing.

In addition, human psychology shows its bad side here too. People often fail to repay even such loans on time, which leads to fines and additional problems. If a student nevertheless sits down to write his thesis in the last week, then the person who took out the loan simply will not have the incentive to pay everything on time. In addition, an interest-free loan for a year provides for a stable financial position during this period. But we know that there is never stability in the economy.

Hopefully, you will be able to avoid many of the bad financial habits mentioned above. Create your financial plan and strictly follow it - this will allow you to be conscious about your finances.

13

Financial Literacy

This is not a very simple question, because different people understand it differently, and this concept itself is rather philosophical and purely subjective. But if we still try to give direction to our course, then we can say that:

Financial literacy is a clear understanding of how money works, how to earn it and manage it. There are two main characteristics of a financially literate person. First: his expenses never exceed his income. Second: any positive difference between monthly income and expenses is used in investments of any form.

Surely you know many people who have been earning quite good money for several years and yet are barely making ends meet. They are great at what they do. It could be programming, art, science, sports . However, some of them even manage to get into debt . And it would be nice if they bought themselves important things with the help of which they develop . Typically, these products are completely pointless and purchasing them becomes burdensome.

FINANCIAL OUTLOOK

This may seem strange, but it doesn't matter how much you earn at the moment. In the history of mankind, there are thousands of stories about how a completely poor person became a millionaire. There are also reverse stories: people who were hit with wealth managed to lose everything in a short time. Therefore, it is very important to understand that your current income is not a death sentence. This is precisely why financial literacy is needed. It shows how, by acquiring some financial habits, anyone can climb out of a financial hole and get back on their feet.

Economics is a difficult tool to understand. This is evidenced by financial crises when even the best economists in the world were not able to predict things that now seem obvious. Now economists use the phrase about cycles, abdicating responsibility: "There are cycles, there will always be world crises." No one can predict the exact date of the crisis, but everyone can prepare for it.

Can a millionaire be financially illiterate? Maybe. For example, this is a Hollywood actor who can receive several million dollars for one role. After some time, his fame fades, and with it, his financial condition disappears. Therefore, he is forced to spend the rest of his life playing low-paying roles, selling off his property to make ends meet. This is a perfect illustration of the importance of financial literacy.

Studying the theory, and cultivating a conscious attitude towards money and financial thinking - these three things will help any person get settled in life.

Financial thinking is most important, but it is very important to constantly learn and supplement knowledge with practical skills. Some people believe that you need to work as hard as possible to become financially secure. On the one hand, this is true, but on the other hand, you must, first of all, work wisely. Once you start your financial journey, you are forced to work as hard as possible. But there is one important point: the more money you have, the more intelligently you should approach your work.

Remember that you can apply financial knowledge now. Everything you do with your finances today affects your future. When you stop buying things you don't need, you have new opportunities. A simple thought begins to form in your mind - money should make new money. Simply spending your income gives immediate results and does not move you forward in any way.

No one is born financially literate. You can be born into a rich family, but this does not guarantee you a wonderful financial future.

To develop a financial mindset, you need to spend many months on it. However, you can develop many positive changes in yourself within a few days. The theory of money can be learned fairly quickly, and it is also relatively easy to understand how the stock market or bank works. Only by understanding how finance works will you begin to move forward little by little.

In past times, financial literacy was even worse. The man was forced to work from morning to night to at least survive. Financial culture existed in its infancy. To become a wealthy person, you had to use force. Nowadays, a lot has changed, and this is a great chance for each of us to succeed in life. There are a lot of freely available materials: books, courses, and videos. Any information is available here and now. However, as we know, the availability of information at the same time depreciates it. You must clearly understand that you already have everything you need for financial prosperity, you just need to find the right materials.

Perhaps the most important skill for developing financial literacy is discipline. More than 90% of people in the world spend money completely thoughtlessly, and it is for this reason that none of them will become wealthy people. Nobody guarantees anything to the remaining 10%, but they still have more chances. By developing discipline around your financial habits, you increase your chances a thousandfold of being retired in ten years, having passive sources of income, and doing whatever you want.

14

Personal Budget Management Tips

Being a financially literate person not only in work and business, but also in everyday life is very important, necessary and useful. One of the basic banking rules says that if financial matters are in order, then everything is in order. We all earn and spend money, sometimes we save, sometimes we plan purchases. But in most cases, we manage our money as we have to, guided only by general rules, which often leads to the need to spend savings, if any, borrow money or even take out loans. To this we can also add the fact that, according to financial experts, about 20% of funds regularly disappear from the budget, the management of which is not given due attention, "somewhere" (it is only unknown where). How can we talk about financial stability here, not to mention financial independence?

Today, a huge amount of literature has been written on the topic of competent budgeting, many training courses have been created, and various trainings and seminars are held. But, unfortunately, not everyone has the time (and money) to study the relevant materials and courses. And agree, how nice it would be if you could just read one article that would briefly, competently and concisely outline the basic principles of managing and controlling personal finances? We hasten to congratulate you - this is exactly the article in front of you! And believe me, after reading it, managing your personal budget will become much easier for you.

What is Budget?

So what is a budget? A budget is a document (electronic or paper) in which all items of income and expenses for a specific period of time are regularly visually and in detail displayed, i.e. all sources of inflow of funds, all expenses, as well as any individual rules for managing finances and a personal financial plan for the future. To a person who has never been seriously involved in budget management, at first glance this may seem like a complicated process, requiring some special knowledge or skills, a huge amount of time, etc. In fact, there is nothing difficult about it for the simple reason that it is just a skill that just needs to be mastered. Budgeting includes several basic parts, which are supplemented with others over time, acquiring the features of a more complex system. But you always need to start with the simplest. The main components of maintaining a personal budget are:

- Accounting for income and expenses
- Cost optimization
- Planning income and expenses

Remember that you need to manage your budget in exactly this order, because... each subsequent point is a logical continuation of the previous one. Let's consider each of them separately.

Accounting for income and expenses

Income accounting is necessary so that, firstly, you clearly know where every penny comes from in your wallet, and secondly, what specific amount is your monthly income. Since a year consists of 12 months, and the source of income for the vast majority of people is wages, then we will continue to charge one month for a "specific time period".

But if the situation with income is quite simple: received - recorded, received - recorded, etc., then with expenses the situation is somewhat different.

As already mentioned, 20% of the income of many people who do not manage their budget "disappears." Moreover, this happens even in cases where it seems that you know exactly what you are spending your money on. And this amount could be used wisely: spent on something significant and truly necessary, or postponed. You can "return" this money, but until you know where it "disappears", you will not be able to do this. This is the first reason why you need to keep track of expenses. And you need to do this every day.

Get yourself a separate notebook and always carry it with you. To begin with, spend money in your usual way, as you are used to. But be sure to record all your expenses, even if it is 7.5 rubles for a cake or 2 rubles for a box of matches. Divide the sheets of the expense notebook into two parts - "purchase name" and "amount". Place dates at the top of the sheets. Don't categorize your purchases - this is unnecessary now, just write them down, because... your main task is to develop such a habit and determine the reason for the "disappearance" of money. You shouldn't rely on your memory in this matter either, because... the very next day you will diligently remember what you spent on.

Check the remaining money against your notes weekly to check that your entries are accurate and systematic, and to see if there is anything on your list that you could give up without causing significant harm to yourself. You might be surprised to learn that such things exist. At the end of the month, count all such expenses and determine their total amount - this way you will get the desired result, i.e. Finally, you will find out where one fifth of all your money is regularly spent. Now you can henceforth refrain from such expenses and direct the "found" money in another direction.

In addition, regular entries in a notebook after each purchase will automatically force you to think about the feasibility of the purchase, which means you will approach your expenses more consciously. After 2-3 months of this practice, having already gotten used to it, you can divide your expenses into categories (food, transportation, utilities, entertainment, etc.).

Cost optimization

Cost optimization implies rational use of funds. And this is by no means saving money. Saving is the abandonment of what is pleasant, familiar and enjoyable in favor of what is necessary in order to save money. Optimization is the competent distribution of personal financial flows across all items of one's expenses without the need to deny oneself anything essential. You may have to give up something, but it will be so insignificant that, in fact, it will not even be felt. Cost optimization is based on the following principles, which are very important to understand:

There are no expense items that are not important to you. To spend less, you should reduce each item in proportion to each other, i.e. deduct funds from each item in the same percentage.

Those expense items that require the greatest amount of funds from your budget are subject to the greatest optimization, because... their costs can most likely be reduced.

There is no need to strive to purchase things advertised as economical, or to purchase in bulk. The human psyche is structured in such a way that due to the apparent cheapness or supposed discount, he will unconsciously strive to take more, which means that he will spend more.

Once you know exactly your basic and real needs and determine how best to optimize expenses, you can begin distributing funds according to goals and time periods. For example, having received a salary, set aside part of the money for basic expenses (mandatory payments), leave the other part (even if very small) as savings, and divide the remaining amount into the four weeks that make up the month. Separate these four parts from each other, placing them, for example, in envelopes. Open each new envelope only on the eve of the coming week. The less money in each of these envelopes, the more disciplined and rational you will be in your spending. And one more useful tip: the more prone you are to thoughtless purchases, the less money it is recommended to carry with you during the day.

The above practice is actually very effective. If you stick to it for at least six months, you will learn to save decent amounts of money, and also develop a useful habit of spending money only on what is really necessary, while not only not worsening, but also improving the quality of your life.

15

Mutual Funds

Playing on the stock exchange can make almost anyone bankrupt or a millionaire. It is the desire to become a rich person that is a strong motivation to study the stock market. However, the larger the amount you want to receive, the greater the risks. Mutual funds are designed to reduce this risk, but in this case the profit will not be so cosmic. Let us consider in this article what mutual funds are and what they are like.

A mutual fund or mutual fund is a portfolio of shares selected and purchased by professional financiers with the investments of thousands of small investors. In this way, the investor reduces risk because his investment is spread across a large number of different businesses.

Investors (that is, you) are called shareholders, and the share of the fund that you purchase is called a unit.

On the stock exchange there is a huge chance of going broke very quickly, which is why mutual funds are so popular. This is not a new invention: the first mutual fund was created in the United

States in 1924. Playing on the stock exchange, even for experienced investors, is something like a casino. The exchange is quite chaotic and unpredictable and few people even understand the rules of the game. But those who understand become billionaires, like Warren Buffett.

Types of Mutual Funds

There are two types of mutual funds: open-end and closed-end.

An open-end mutual fund issues new shares (units) and buys them back from shareholders. It also has the following features:

The price of a unit depends only on the fundamental indicators of the fund's assets.
Units are sold and purchased only through the fund.

An unlimited number of shares can be issued.
Units are traded at a price equal to the net asset value per unit. Net asset is the value of the fund's net assets divided by the number of shares (units).

A closed-end mutual fund issues a limited number of shares (units) and does not repurchase them from shareholders. It has the following features:

- The price of a unit depends on the fundamental indicators of the fund's assets and the ratio of supply and demand in the market.
- Units are traded on stock exchanges.
- A limited number of shares are issued.
- Units may trade at a price above, below or equal to the net asset value per unit.

Based on asset type, mutual funds are divided into stock funds, bond funds, balanced income funds, money market funds and real estate funds.

Let's look at four steps to investing in these funds.

Investing in Mutual Funds

Select a financial institution

You can choose a huge number of such institutions, because there are a lot of people willing to manage your finances. If your funds are quite limited, you can try to invest the money yourself. In this case, you will need to study everything yourself and carefully monitor the placement and results of your investments.

If your capital allows, you can hire a financial advisor. Such people take a substantial amount for their work plus interest on their income.

Remember that you should not focus on funds that performed well a year or two ago. These indicators may not be current.

Determine the risk

Even mutual funds have some risk. In addition, they have varying degrees of risk: from low to high. You can find risk ratings for each mutual fund on financial websites. Typically, this is a scale from 1 to 5. The greater the risk, the greater the reward is likely to be.

You can invest a small amount of money in a very risky fund and the rest of your money in a less risky one.

Invest in different funds

Diversification of investments is extremely important for successful investing. Experienced investors advise investing in assets of different classes. These could be equity funds for enterprises in your country or other countries, funds in specific industries (real estate, agriculture), bond funds. This way you will not be subject to fluctuations in the development of a particular industry. Remember the golden rule of business: "Don't put all your eggs in one basket." It has to do with risks. Spread the risks.

Don't try to predict market developments

This is an incredibly difficult task even for experienced investors. Although you can study the market and its trends. Invest for the long term (more than five years) - this way the short-term ups and downs of the market won't have a big impact on you.

16

Convert your Abilities into Money

In 1949, Earl Prewett, a sales professional and successful author, wrote a book called "How to Turn Your Ability Into Cash." The book contains step-by-step instructions for turning your abilities and ideas into money. These are the recommendations Prewett makes in it.

Intelligence, according to Prewett, is the ability to pull oneself together, evaluate one's abilities and environment to look for opportunities, create a work plan, and take action. It's a five-step process:

1. Summarize.
2. Pay attention to your environment and look for opportunities.
3. Create a plan to identify the opportunity.
4. Develop a process to put the plan into action.
5. Take action!

Let's look at each step in more detail.

Summarize

The first step is to take stock. That is, take an inventory of your qualities, skills and abilities. Ask yourself the following questions:

- What do you find significant about yourself?
- What do you like to do?
- When was the last time you were so engrossed in an activity that it felt like time stood still?
- What are your skills and talents?
- What experience do you have?
- What skills have you already invested time and energy into?
- What problems can you solve?

As Prewett explains, the most interesting thing in the world is you. The problem is that you haven't taken the time to evaluate yourself, analyze your capabilities, fully realize your strengths, and figure out what kind of interesting person you are. But you need to make an effort to find out.

Step Two: Pay Attention to Your Environment and Look for Opportunities

The second step is to use your power of observation to take stock of the environment in which you live. What opportunities do you see? What need is unmet? What problems need to be solved?

The result of observation is inspiration and enthusiasm, a tendency to new discoveries and a desire to improve any existing plan or subject.

Here are three examples of Prewett's use of the power of observation:

Robert Fulton sat in his mother's kitchen and watched the steam rise from the tea pot. "He has power. I will use it," he said. The result of this was the steam engine.

Charles Goodyear watched the mixture cook on the stove. It overflowed and froze in an elastic mass. Thanks to this observation, he later created rubber.

Step Three: Create a Plan to Address the Opportunity You've Identified

The third step in the process of turning your ability into money is to create a plan that will allow you to take advantage of the opportunity.

Write down how you can apply your experience, knowledge, and skills to solve the problem you identified in step two of this process. A plan gives an idea, an image formed in the mind.

Ask yourself:

- What you need?
- Do you want to sell something?
- Do you want to find a job?
- Do you want a salary increase?
- Do you want more clients?
- Are you trying to invent something?

The only way to realize your desire is with a plan. Every word, every thought and every sentence must have its place. A plan is organized knowledge to describe the reasons why a dream should become a reality.

Create your plan by gathering all the facts and learning everything you can about what you want. Collect data, organize it and classify it. Then convert it into a plan.

Present this plan sequentially, list each point step by step and try to use words with pictures. Use concrete terms in your plan rather than abstract phrases.

Step Four: Develop a Process to Put the Plan into Action

The fourth step is to develop a process to put the plan you created into action. In other words, set up a process for implementing the plan.

At this stage you need to use 4 laws.

Law of Faith : Faith is the belief in a favorable outcome of any undertaking. Faith gives life, strength and moves the plan forward. Faith inspires you to have absolute confidence in your plan and gives you the strength to turn ideas into money.

Law of Repetition : You have learned everything in your life with the help of this law. You improve your plan through the law of repetition. Every time you review your plan, you learn something new. You develop inspiration, gain enthusiasm.

Law of Imagination : Imagination is the mastery of the mind. You begin to develop your idea using your imagination. Prewett says that in 1886, an old doctor, John Pemberton, created the formula. He didn't know what to do with it, but he believed it was important. He told a young clerk he knew about this formula and explained its content. He bought it.

He later found out that the formula described the composition of an excellent refreshing drink, which he began to produce. This is how Coca-Cola was born.

Law of Persistence : You can believe in an idea, repeat and improve it, use your imagination, but without persistence you will get nowhere. You must demonstrate persistence. To persevere, you need to resolutely continue to implement your plan, despite all adversities.

Act, act, act

The last step is to take action to make the plan a reality. Applying what you know reveals many things you don't know about. Therefore, at this stage it is important not only to act, but also to learn quickly. Follow your plan, but be prepared to change it.

17

10 mistakes of a New Entrepreneur

It's not entirely correct to talk about what a novice entrepreneur should do. There is neither a general law of success for business , nor separate recipes for each of its possible areas that would always work without fail. But the experience and empirical material accumulated over the years allows us to talk about what those who have decided to open their own business should definitely not do. Of course, you can acquire wisdom by stepping on all the mistakes yourself, but it is better to use the formula of O. von Bismarck: "Only fools learn from their own experience. I prefer to learn from the experiences of others."

1. Underestimating the experience of others

It often happens that a person reads the biographies of great businessmen (J. Rockefeller, G. Ford, S. Jobs) and is inspired by their successes. It's interesting to read about ups and downs; moreover, they motivate . The other side is hard work , overcoming failures, mistakes made play the role of episodes and often go unnoticed. We forget how things really are - that success means months, or even years of preparation behind the screen, and only an hour in the spotlight. Based on this, it is worth remembering that you always need to analyze someone else's experience in two planes – "what worked" and "failure". The second one is often even more useful, although much less is written about it.

1. **Hope to sell the idea**

Investors very rarely invest in ideas. Investments are a business just like what you do. Would you yourself invest money in a product that does not yet exist? Therefore, when trying to find funding, you should, at a minimum, have a prototype and several hundred pre-orders for it. Better yet, a working model has already been sold to a certain number of people. It is clear that this is just an example, the essence of which boils down to the fact that it is very difficult to sell something that does not exist. To do this, you must have at least strong evidence that the idea is needed at all.

1. **Trying to make everything perfect**

In other words – the notorious perfectionism. This mistake is briefly described by the famous saying: "The best is the enemy of the good." Many startups remain at the implementation stage of their first project because they spent too long trying to "smooth out the corners." As a result, it either failed because it was impossible, and they lost a lot of time, or competitors from among other enthusiasts did it even worse, but faster. And they only remember the one who was first. Nowadays this statement is especially true. Therefore, it is very important to understand that it is impossible to make a perfect product in all respects. No matter how good the iPad is, it does not change the fact that millions of people prefer tablets from Samsung and many other manufacturers.

1. **Start a business to make money**

This will be your goal in any case, otherwise opening your own business loses all meaning. But here we are talking about creating a business not with the sole purpose of making a profit, but also with the goal of solving a problem. In other words, as experts note, it is very difficult to build a long-term strong business by trying to make money "on the wave", on trendy items and phenomena. The more successful companies are those that are not driven by the search for a niche where they can make quick money, but think of the product as a tool, passion, hobby. Often they are the ones who create something that changes the idea of the world.

1. **Creating the product or service you want**

Today it is no longer a secret to anyone that the market lives according to its own objective principles and laws. Therefore, when starting to implement your idea, think about how the buyer will react to it. Will he be interested in your offer? Are you delivering exactly what the market needs? Otherwise, by doing what you want and what only you like, you risk "burning out." Even industry giants spend millions annually on market research. It is clear that you will not have that kind of money at your disposal at the stage of creating a business, but you will certainly have friends and the opportunity to use the Internet. This is already enough to, with a skillful approach, determine how potential buyers will react to your product or service.

FINANCIAL OUTLOOK

1. **All attention to money**

"Where can I get money?" is a global issue that concerns all budding entrepreneurs. Expense items can be different: hiring specialists, renting production space, purchasing, logistics and much more. This is all very important. But focusing on money alone is wrong. In business, the ability to find and use other resources is not the least important. When renowned entrepreneur MJ Gottlieb became a licensed partner of Samsung America, he did not receive a dime from the Korean company. But he had at his disposal production facilities, the best accountants, a sales network and everything else belonging to the technology giant.

1. **Personnel policy and cooperation**

Finding good specialists for a project that is at the beginning of its journey is not an easy task. Not everyone will share your ideals or approach your work with the same enthusiasm as you. You should be prepared for this. But in no case should you approach this issue without the proper degree of attention. Check the people you will be working with. Choose partners and suppliers not only based on the price of their services. One more thing. It is very common for us to recruit relatives and friends into business. This is bad practice. D. Ogilvy wrote that only after stepping on the rake several times on his own, he was convinced that it was impossible to hire his relatives or relatives of clients for work. Firstly, it is more difficult to fire them if they cannot cope with the job. Secondly, even if they are better than everyone else, you will not get rid of conversations about how it is their bosses who promote them up the career ladder and forgive everything. In such conditions it is difficult to create a strong team . Thirdly, by firing such an employee, you will jeopardize your relationship with him or the client.

1. **Underestimating competition**

Young projects often tend to describe their idea as one that has no analogues, and therefore has no competitors. This is mistake. Something truly unique is created very rarely. Even if there is nothing on the market today similar to what you plan to produce, it is not a fact that it will not appear tomorrow. Market analysis will help in this regard even if someone has previously tried to implement a similar idea, but for various reasons failed. In other words, you should ask yourself not only how strong your competitors are, but also figure out what the reason is if there are practically none.

1. **Lack of focus**

It often happens that, in search of his place in the market, a young entrepreneur grabs onto several ideas at once and works on their development in parallel. Dmitry Alimov, a Russian entrepreneur and managing partner of Frontier Ventures, says this approach is unacceptable. "In the eyes of an investor, the lack of focus suggests that the team doesn't really believe in any of these projects. People scatter their time and effort chasing several birds with one stone, which significantly reduces the chances of success, since focused teams usually win. As someone who has built several businesses myself as an entrepreneur, I believe that a truly serious opportunity cannot be pursued half-heartedly."

1. Sacrificing the client for profit

Having reached a certain level of development, the question arises about further expansion of the business. The main thing here is to avoid making a number of mistakes. A radical change in the positioning of a product or an improvement in service coupled with a sharp increase in prices can make your loyal audience turn away from you. Even well-known companies have made similar mistakes. For example, Oldsmobile, a manufacturer of cars that were positioned as cars for middle-aged and elderly people. In the wake of interest in retro, this division of GM released advertising to young people that was supposed to make their cars look "cool." It was not successful - the advertisement remained misunderstood by young people. What's even worse is that some of the previous customers left, which is why sales among the target audience fell.

18

Financial Problem and their Solution

It often happens that you ignore some financial problems that usually arise during the most difficult moments of everyday life. But, as soon as they appear, they need to be resolved, because a delay in time can lead to the formation of debts that you will not be able to get rid of so easily.

Below we will tell you how to solve financial problems without creating debt traps.

1. **Having debts**

There were definitely days or months when debts arose, which, perhaps even at the moment, have not yet been closed. Of course, some people get them back faster, while others still get stuck with them or can't get rid of them at all. Debt often results from poor personal budget management. If you find yourself in this situation, then it's time to force yourself to pay off current debts and not create new ones. Set aside 5% - 7% of your salary monthly to pay off debts. This way you will gradually close them.

1. **Lack of money for emergencies**

A toothache, a broken appliance, or a wedding invitation may be one of the situations that arises unexpectedly and requires additional costs. And since these expenses were not provided for, the question arises: where to get the money? To overcome such situations, it would be a good idea to create an emergency fund in time, where you will save a certain amount of money every month. And if you still don't have time to do this, then a quick loan from CreditPrime will certainly help you out.

1. **Expenses exceed income**

Compare your monthly income and expenses. You should have a positive difference. If there is nothing left from your monthly income, then you need to take a detailed look at what you are spending your money on and cut down on your expenses to make a positive difference and start saving. Create a document in which you track your money. Indicate monthly fixed and one-time expenses. Try to reduce spending on less important purchases. You can also try to save on electricity or gas. Maybe you should limit going out with friends to cafes and drink coffee at home.

1. **Impulsive decisions about money**

Various promotions always tempt most people to make impulse

purchases. Satisfying your cravings isn't a bad thing, but first, we recommend carefully analyzing your personal budget and considering how useful this purchase will be for you. Be more disciplined and avoid impulse purchases, especially if you are not in the mood or are afraid of missing out on an offer. This way you will save not only money, but also nerves.

1. **Failure to save money**

The concept of saving money is known to everyone, but, unfortunately, not everyone manages to save money. However, it would still be a good idea to do this because money from savings can cover not only unexpected expenses, but also personal pleasures such as a long-awaited trip or buying a new smartphone. Anything is possible, you just need to set a goal to save money every month. Open a savings account and immediately transfer 3% - 5% to this account on the day you receive your salary. Start with small amounts, and then, when the habit is formed, you will automatically want to save even more.

Solution of Financial Problem

There are situations when you have to stay at home: illness, quarantine, social isolation due to coronavirus, or simply bad weather. But life doesn't have to stop - it can move online, at least partially. We offer 10 tips on how to save time, energy and health while receiving financial and other services remotely.

1. **Set up automatic payments for yourself and your loved ones**

Older people are accustomed to paying bills at bank offices. But during epidemics there is no need to take risks. Connect yourself, your parents, and grandparents to automatic payment for housing and communal services, mobile communications and the Internet, taxes and fines.

You can set up many automatic payments through the Government Services Portal, your personal account or your bank's mobile application, as well as on the websites of service provider companies.

1. **Order everything to your home**

To avoid going to supermarkets and pet stores, order food and groceries for animals at home. Many chain supermarkets, from economical to luxury, have established delivery of goods.

If you can't go outside, you can do something useful or enjoyable at home. For example, prepare your favorite dish according to your grandmother's recipe, which you usually don't have time for, dismantle the mezzanine or update the interior. Construction materials, furniture and household appliances are also delivered to your home.

1. **Practice good cyber hygiene**

Cyber fraudsters often create duplicate websites of well-known online stores and services. Fake addresses may differ from real ones by just one or two characters. On fake websites, criminals steal personal information and card details using phishing . Carefully check the addresses of stores and services where you will pay with a card or enter personal data. And save those that you use constantly in your bookmarks.

Get a separate debit card for online purchases. And put on it exactly the amount you are going to spend. Some banks are ready to remotely issue you a regular plastic card and deliver it.

Many banks and electronic payment systems (electronic wallets) offer to issue a special virtual card for payments on the Internet. It has details, but no physical media.

Some virtual cards, also called digital, can be loaded into a smartphone with the NFC function - contactless payment. In this case, the virtual card is also suitable for offline purchases, as well as transfers and receiving cash from ATMs.

1. **Transfer money by phone number**

When you urgently need to send money to friends or family, you can do this, for example, through the Fast Payment System (FPS) . SBP allows you to make instant transfers using a mobile phone number, even if the sender and recipient have accounts in different banks.

From May 1, 2020, all transfers through SBP up to 100,000 rubles per month will become free. If the amount exceeds this limit, banks will have the right to charge a commission of up to 0.5% of the transfer size, but not more than 1,500 rubles. However, some banks have already set zero tariffs for all transfers, without waiting for May 1.

Online purchases can also be made through SBP if the online store has enabled payment via QR code . This is safer than paying by card because you do not need to enter any details on the website.

1. **Apply for loans and deposits remotely**

Most large banks have long transferred their services to a remote format. Through your personal account or mobile application, you can make a deposit or apply for a loan and receive money directly to your card.

It might make sense to get a credit card with a long grace period. It will allow you to use the bank's money and not pay interest for some time. Such a card will help out during a period when income has temporarily decreased.

If your data is in the Unified Biometric System, then you can become a client of other banks without visiting their offices. The most convenient way to select suitable offers is through the website of the Unified Biometric System.

1. **Check your credit history**

If you urgently need money and you are going to apply for a loan or loan, first study your credit history. Through the Public Services Portal you can find out which credit history bureaus (BKI) store it. And then, also remotely, request reports from the BKI.

Credit reports from BKI are issued free of charge twice a year. It's a good idea to order them periodically to make sure your credit history is in order.

1. **Convert money without exchangers**

During periods of financial instability, you should not rush to buy or sell currency just to benefit from exchange rate fluctuations. Even professionals are not always able to predict its movement. Inexperienced people are much more likely to lose money than to make money.

But if the purchase cannot be postponed, there is no need to go to exchange offices. Cash can also be a carrier of infection. Banks, as a rule, allow you to open foreign currency accounts and make conversions through your personal account or mobile application. In addition, exchange rates are usually better online than in bank offices.

1. **Buy insurance online**

Many popular types of insurance, for example, a motor third party liability insurance policy (MTPL), can be purchased without leaving your home - on the websites of insurance companies. Moreover, according to OSAGO, the cost of the policy can be calculated in advance .

Previously, only insurers themselves could issue policies online, but since 2020, intermediaries insurance agents and brokers—have also acquired this right. Before purchasing a policy on the insurance company's website, check its license in the Bank of Russia directory , and a complete list of compulsory motor third party liability insurers can be found on the website of the Russian Union of Auto Insurers . It is more difficult to verify the integrity of agents and brokers.

1. Optimize your budget

Forced seclusion can be used to get your finances in order. Analyze your expenses for two to three months: categorize them to understand what you spend the most on. Evaluate what unnecessary expenses you can give up - temporarily or forever.

Think about your long-term goals and create a financial plan . It may have to be postponed for some time. But it is always useful to have clear guidelines.

1. Improve financial literacy

Many educational portals, libraries, even video services offer free or inexpensive access to their resources. Use this opportunity not only for fun, but also for learning. For example, to learn something new in the professional field and increase your value as a specialist.

And financial literacy skills will be useful to absolutely everyone. Read our articles, for example, about financial planning and investing . Or take part in free webinars for private investors or entrepreneurs. Difficult times will pass, but the knowledge will remain with you.

19

How to Overcome the Fear of Failure and Develop a Growth Mentality

Millions of people suffer from this condition. Emotional symptoms include feelings of powerlessness, anxiety, panic and fear. This is atychiphobia , but most people call it fear of failure and it is largely instinctive. We are naturally risk-averse—scientists call this the desire for safety .

In today's world, we rarely face physical risks, and as a result, our brains try to protect us from things like embarrassment and failure. Our ability to tolerate discomfort, even emotional discomfort, is so low that most of us would rather eliminate all risks than take an alternative path that might bring greater benefits. But choosing the safest options is riskier than you think . To succeed, we must change the way we think about failure.

The Need for Failure

Google, one of the most innovative companies in history, tried to identify the most important characteristics of successful teams. Their research, called Project Aristotle , reached many people. What did you find out? Psychological safety turned out to be the most important feature of the most effective teams:

> **"In a team with a high level of psychological safety, members feel confident when they have to take risks in each other's presence. They know that none of their colleagues will judge or punish them for making a mistake, asking a question, or proposing an idea."**

So there is a clear connection between innovation and willingness to fail. In this era of change, companies that refuse to take risks fall behind competitors or go bankrupt. It is essential for survival that risk taking is an integral part of an organization's culture. There are many examples in modern history of giant corporations dying out like dinosaurs due to lack of innovation.

Some of the most brilliant minds have not only prepared for failure, but welcomed it.

> "In my company, failure is an option. If you don't have failures, you're not innovative enough." Elon Musk

> "It's great to celebrate success, but it's more important to learn from failure." Bill Gates

"You have to be ready to take action. You have to be prepared for failure

and failure, otherwise you won't achieve much." Steve Jobs

The Importance of Mentality

Babe Ruth is one of the greatest baseball players of all time. He was admired by millions of fans from around the world. Even people who are indifferent to baseball may know that he set the record for most home runs . But did you know that he also set the record for most strikeouts ?

"The batter had to defend the house, hit the ball, as in the related game of cricket," writes biographer Robert Creamer in his book Babe: The Legend Comes to Life .

"But for Root, the strike was a momentary, albeit disappointing, setback. Protecting his home wasn't a big deal to him." His style of play completely overturned the established ideas about baseball. In an instant, he changed the game, making it what we know it today.

"Every strike brings me closer to the next home run," Babe Ruth once admitted. For Babe, failure was the tool he used to achieve success.

"Until you begin to see failure in a positive way, your people will not strive to make significant changes," says Charlene Lee , lead analyst at Prophet-owned Altimeter. But to accept failure and see it as an integral part of team performance, you need to change your mindset. Failure should not be seen as a sequence of failures, but as a competitive advantage. In his book "The New Psychology of Success. Think and Win," Carol Dweck identified two types of thinking: a fixed mindset and a growth mentality :

A fixed mindset prevents growth and learning, while a growth mentality helps you perceive failure in a positive way and use it to move forward.

How to overcome the fear of failure and develop a growth mentality in your organization

1. **Take advantage of every opportunity to learn**

Celebrate failure because it gives you an opportunity to learn a valuable lesson. After each project, get together with the team and discuss what experience can be used in the future. Encourage participants to share which factors worked and which did not. If people are hesitant to share their opinions, start by discussing what you would like to improve on your next project.

It is your responsibility as a manager or leader to minimize risks. Help the team understand that you can't insure against everything. A series of small failures will help you avoid a major failure in the future. This does not mean that we should strive for them. But it is important to remember that you learn from mistakes.

1. **Exchange feedback**

Feedback is very necessary to adjust your actions. The more often you get them, the better for everyone. Regularly ask for feedback from team members and provide feedback yourself whenever possible. By demonstrating your willingness to receive feedback, you set the tone for the entire team so that no one is embarrassed to speak their mind. When everyone learns to give honest feedback, it will become easier for them to receive it.

If you receive constructive feedback, take it into account and let the reviewer know you took advantage of their suggestions. People will be more willing to share honest feedback if it produces results. Please note that feedback should not be limited to criticism.

1. **Praise the process**

When things go well, the performers are usually praised for it. But it's more important to praise the process that led you to success. According to Carol Dweck, "If you believe that intelligence can be developed with some effort, then you are more likely to have a positive attitude toward such effort."

Even if the project did not end the way you would like, still look for factors that you can comment on. Emphasize the team members' level of motivation, praise team members' teamwork and commitment to getting things done, or say a few words about team members' perseverance. This will help your employees not to give up and tune in for the best.

1. **Fight groupthink**

When the fear of failure increases, people begin to hide their thoughts and opinions. They will not strive to change the situation for the better, but to avoid mistakes. The best ideas do not come out of nowhere, but are chosen from many others - both successful and unsuccessful. To ensure that brainstorming works, give your employees time to generate new ideas. The point is for each participant to come up with a dozen ideas from which you can choose.

Encourage divergent thinking and, when solving problems, try to take your time. Well, if a decision is made too quickly, push team members to think as big as possible. Appoint someone to be the devil's advocate. His task will be to challenge the most popular ideas and the flawlessness of the plan. And remember: diversity of opinion can be your greatest strength, so strive for it. Be sure to give each participant an opportunity to speak.

1. **Encourage employee development**

As a manager, it is your responsibility to provide your subordinates with opportunities for learning and development. Emphasize the skills of each team member and treat them as resources that others can use. Not only will this have a positive impact on team cohesion, but it will also make people want to live up to high expectations and help others.

Mentoring is something that every team member should do. Let them regularly share their knowledge, especially lessons learned from mistakes. By doing so, you can learn from failure and help your employees grow and develop.

Together we make mistakes and together we win

At Wrike we have three core values : growth, action and collaboration. Living by these values has helped us develop a culture of growth and conquer the fear of failure.

Growth

A growth mentality helps us overcome challenges and innovate. We set ambitious goals that help us move forward with each new quarter. We strive for better all the time.

Action

We, unlike many teams, don't spend time thinking about how things might turn out. And minor failures don't stop us. We put all our strength into work and achieving goals.

Collaboration

Each of us has something to share and teach, and we believe that collaboration is the key to our success. We use each other's strengths, and this helps us on the way to our goals. We make mistakes together and win together.

It may seem counterintuitive, but the most important thing a team can do to stay safe is to take risks. Working together, supporting our desire to grow, and helping each other overcome the consequences of our mistakes has been key to our development and can similarly transform your team. By freeing yourself from the fear of failure and developing a growth mentality, you are on the path to success.

20

Review Request

Dear Readers,

I am thrilled to invite you to share your thoughts on *"Financial Outlook:* **A Beginner Guide to Economics Independence***"* Your feedback is invaluable in shaping the journey of this book and providing insights for future readers.

In this book we begin on a transformative exploration of the intricate relationship between mindset and financial success. I would love to hear how the book resonated with you, whether it sparked a mindset shift, provided actionable insights, or offered clarity on navigating the complex landscape of personal finance.

Your reviews contribute not only to the growth of this book but also to the broader community seeking financial empowerment. Share your experiences, highlight the chapters that resonated most with you, and let others know how "Financial Mindset 101" has influenced your approach to money matters.

If you found the book valuable, your review could be the encouragement

REVIEW REQUEST

someone needs to begin on their own journey towards financial enlightenment. Alternatively, if there are areas you believe could be enhanced, your constructive feedback will be instrumental in refining future editions.

Thank you for taking the time to share your thoughts and join the conversation on cultivating a smart financial mindset. Your reviews are a crucial part of this collective learning experience.

Warm regards,

Jorden Beacon

www.ingramcontent.com/pod-product-compliance
Lightning Source LLC
Chambersburg PA
CBHW050100230526
45470CB00004B/1618